UNLONELY PLANET

UNLONELY PLANET

JILLIAN RICHARDSON

NEW DEGREE PRESS

UNLONELY PLANET

ISBN 978-1-64137-260-2 *Paperback*

978-1-64137-261-9 *Ebook*

For my chosen family

CONTENTS

*"This is the power of gathering: it inspires us,
delightfully, to be more hopeful, more joyful,
more thoughtful: in a word, more alive."*

—ALICE WATERS

December 26, 2015 was my first day living in New York City. I stood on the sidewalk and looked fondly at the dirty building that was my new home. I was an adult! I was in the East Village!

This big moment, which also included me quietly singing "Welcome to New York" by Taylor Swift, was interrupted by my mom, who screamed as a rat calmly walked over her foot. I was not fazed. She was.

Understandably, my parents were not thrilled that this rodent-infested place was my first home outside of college. Nevertheless, they helped me move into my fourth-story walk-up, treated me to dinner, and left me to unpack the rest of my things.

I could not have been more thrilled to get them out of there.

Sitting on my twin bed, surrounded by stuff that I soon realized would not fit into my tiny room, I eagerly texted a friend. A few days prior, he'd promised to take me out for my first real night in NYC. I hopped in the shower, buzzing with the anticipation of my initiation into New York life.

When I emerged from the bathroom—which literally had flecks of dirt painted into the tub—I saw that my friend still hadn't responded. I dried my hair. Put on makeup. No response. Changed my clothes. Changed my clothes again. No response. And then—two hours plus a few follow-up texts later—I still hadn't received a message back.

Ugh.

Suddenly, the elated balloon in my chest felt like it was ripped open, filled with concrete, and dropped into my stomach.

It hit me all at once. I had zero close friends in New York, no job, and no clue what I was going to do with myself. All I knew was that I wanted to be a comedy writer... and I didn't have a plan for how to get there either. In that moment, I became hyperaware of the fact that my support system was nonexistent.

As I tried to fall asleep—a neighbor's salsa music bumping outside of my window—I was hit with a familiar feeling: I am deeply alone, and I'm powerless to do anything about it. I have no one to share this moment with.

After barely sleeping, reading my lease to see if it was breakable, and contemplating what I could tell my parents in order to head back to Connecticut, I woke up determined to reframe things in a more positive way.

"I don't need other people's permission to grab NYC by its beautiful, grimy hands!" I told myself. "I'm going to make the most out of this experience. I'm going to have an adventure!"

So, here's what I did in my first week of being a New Yorker:

- Went thrift shopping
- Made a new friend and went to a dive bar
- Took a yoga class in a clothing store
- Visited the Brooklyn museum
- Downloaded Tinder and went on a date
- Saw a comedy show
- Signed up for improv class at the Upright Citizens Brigade
- Joined a gym and worked out
- Filled out four job applications
- Got hired to write reviews of Off-Off-Broadway shows
- Saw my first Off-Off-Broadway show
- Googled "how to write play reviews."

Sounds awesome, right? From then on, every week was packed with new experiences.

Who's lonely? Not me! I got this.

And yet... I didn't feel better. I felt busier, but not more connected. In fact, I might have felt emptier.

Sure, I had filled up every minute in my calendar and was surrounded by people. Yet at the same time, it felt like no one really cared or understood who I was. And I had no idea who I could turn to with that pain.

Yet rather than wallow in self-pity, I stuck with my "I don't need anyone" attitude and continued to attend events, festivals, and retreats all by myself.

In one week I would meet more new people than I had in my last six months of college combined. Yet somehow, I never felt filled up by the connections I made. I still felt like I didn't have anyone to rely on.

Looking back on that time in my life, I now understand that I hungered for more than companionship.

Yes, I was lonely. Yet this feeling was rooted in something even deeper and more primal than a need for conversation. What I really desired was intimacy and to feel like I belonged. In order to make that happen, I needed to fundamentally change my social life. This realization, which led to me finally finding my people, is the backbone of this book.

I had to create my own congregation.

Before you panic and slam this sacrilegious paperback shut, let me assure you that I am not here to preach a made-up faith. I will not propose that I, or Arianna Grande, or a ball of string that I found under my couch will save you. (Although how convenient would that be, right?) However, I will argue that intentionally congregating with others in a healthy way can.

For all of this to make sense, I should back up and explain a bit about America's religious landscape right now. You see, 39 percent of Americans ages eighteen to thirty-nine have no religious affiliation at all. That number has nearly quadrupled from 10 percent in the past 30 years. In America as a whole, 22.8 percent of people are religiously unaffiliated. In addition, 15.8 percent identify as "nothing in particular." This religious makeup is totally different than fifty years ago when most people in the United States relied on a single religious community.[1]

At the same time as attendance in religious services is plummeting in America, loneliness is skyrocketing. The average person in the US only has one close friend. To make things worse, 75 percent of people are not satisfied with their friendships.[2] Bleak, right? To top it off, only 53 percent of people in the US have meaningful in-person social interactions, like an extended conversation with a friend or spending quality time with a family member, on a daily basis.[3] This makes me question what happens in the office, considering the fact that most people spend one-third of their lives at work.[4] Given these statistics, it's clear that our companies are not fostering an environment for forming meaningful relationships.

Yet people being lonely isn't just sad. It's also terrible for our health. Believe it or not, loneliness is just as tied to early mortality as smoking fifteen cigarettes a day, being an excessive drinker, or being obese. Think about how many times your health teacher lectured you about the dangers of binge drinking when you were growing up. Did they ever mention how crucial intimate relationships are for your well-being? Probably not once. They were too busy telling you how having sex will make you get pregnant and die. (Shout-out to *Mean Girls*.)[5]

To summarize all of this in a simple equation: A decrease in the amount of meaningful congregation in America, combined with increased isolation, has resulted in a loneliness epidemic. It's literally killing us, and we're not doing enough to fight it.

The solution? Create consistent, healthy congregations that fulfill us in the way that organized religion used to.

At first glance, that statement is probably confusing. When you read the word "congregation," you typically think of a group of people who gather for religious worship. In fact, if you look in the Webster dictionary, that's pretty much what you'll find. Yet if you flip forward a few pages to "congregate," you'll find something different.

Congregate: *To collect into a group or crowd.*

Were you expecting something cooler? Me too.[6]

So, while it hurts my English major heart to do this, I have to disagree with the dictionary. I believe the act of congregation is about more than people simply existing in the same space. It's about coming together with intention and creating the container for moments of healing, transformation, and community.

When we gather purposefully, we experience a sense of shared humanity. We feel less alone.

Being welcomed into secular congregations has changed my life. These gatherings have given me the space to share what's on my heart, heal from trauma, repair my relationship with my body, and genuinely feel like I matter. While organized religion could have offered me those same benefits, it didn't feel like the right place for me. It still doesn't.

I know many of you feel the same way. And I'm here to tell you, just because you're not gathering around a God doesn't mean you can't feel like you're part of a sacred space that can improve your life. You deserve that feeling, and I hope this book will help you find it.

My friend, singer Tim Victor, once told me, "I don't call myself a gospel singer. I'm a singer. Because church isn't in the building. It's in the people. It's in the feeling of connection. That's the sacredness."

As an adult, I don't belong to any religious institution. Yet I often wish I had a place I could turn to for consistent connection and spiritual growth. While I'm part of communities that I love, these gatherings are all missing some of the key elements of a healthy congregation:

1. They happen every week
2. The same people show up consistently
3. There is space for vulnerable conversation and deep reflection
4. There is mentorship and spiritual guidance, especially from elders
5. There is an easily accessible way for members to give back to the community

This is exactly what organized religions, and healthy congregations in general, excel at.

For example, Bible study provides a space to learn and grow in your connection to a higher power. Coffee after the service allows you to connect with your peers. Volunteering offers the opportunity to give back and feel a sense of fellowship with the congregation. Plus, there's a big bonus. No matter where you move, you can immediately find a place where you share a ritual and similar values.

Like many twenty-something Americans, I don't feel at home in any organized religion. So I have to ask myself, "Where do I belong?"

It took a long time for me to find the answer, but now I have a community that's richer than anything I could have imagined a few years ago. I want to teach others how to find that for themselves and then take the reins to create more spaces that foster this sense of connection.

* * *

Writing this book has been a gift, and it has shown me how good people can be. Aside from combing through tons of research papers, I was lucky enough to talk with a facilitator for a men's group inside of Folsom Prison, an actor in the hit immersive experience *Sleep No More*, and the head of a weekly secular church. I learned what it's like to go from being a pastor to a friendship coach, the head concierge at a Burning Man camp, and a production lead for self-help guru Tony Robbins. I even chatted with a man who can afford an apartment in Soho by teaching business people how to be vulnerable. (Seriously!)

Of course, I also share my own stories in these pages. I dive into how I went from being terrified of dancing to being an honorary producer of the party that helped me get over my fear. I explain what it was like to attend a digital detox summer camp for adults and then work at one. And I also tell how I went from having one close connection in New York City to helping thousands of people be less lonely.

This book is built upon a framework of seven core factors that you can leverage to build or participate in your own congregation. In each chapter, you'll learn about:

1. Getting frientimate
2. Discovering an alternate universe
3. Sharing with strangers
4. Seeking spiritual guidance
5. Finding healing spaces
6. Incorporating ritual
7. Stepping into leadership

If you read no further than this page, know that you're not alone in feeling lonely—and you also hold the power to create the space for rich and rewarding connections in your life.

But if you do continue, I hope this book will become a tool for you. What I have learned in my work with thousands of people like you, as well as my own personal journey, is that there is no singular way to cure loneliness. But the first thing I can do is acknowledge that the problem exists and share how you can do your part to fix it.

I hope I can inspire you to find your people and leave the world a little more connected and loving than it was before.

Right now, this planet is filled with people who feel like they don't matter. They're our neighbors, our lovers, and our friends. This worldwide sense of disconnection is a problem of epic proportions, and one that I've only scratched the surface of.

I'm here hoping this book turns that scratch into a crack, and together we can rip the issue of loneliness wide open.

My main question for *Unlonely Planet* is this: How we can we create secular spaces for healthy congregation? What do they look like and how do they thrive? I'm not going to pretend to have the answers. All I know is that the questions matter, and I'd love to be in conversation with you about them.

Oh, and one last thing... you look really nice today.

Now, onto what you're really here for. The book!

Let's get into it.

1

FINDING MY JOY

"What if depression is, in fact, a form of grief—for our own lives not being as they should? What if it is a form of grief for the connections we have lost, yet still need?"

—JOHANN HARI, LOST CONNECTIONS

In April 2016—just four months after moving to New York City—I received an email that would change my life forever.

The subject line read: "Digital Detox Summer Camp for Adults."

After being curious enough to click through, I was met with this message:

"Camp Grounded is the best Summer Camp for Adults, where grown-ups go to unplug, get away and be kids again. We believe in a world where people are given the freedom, permission, resources and opportunities they need to feel alive, whole, complete and deeply connected to the beauty that is life."

Holy crap. Sign me up.

Their website was filled with images of communal meals, grownups covered in shaving cream throwing cheese puffs at each other, and lots of hugging. Everyone was positively beaming. Looking at the pictures, a thought crossed my mind: "I don't know if I've ever been that happy."

I hit "purchase" on that site because it felt like a solution. Even though my calendar had been completely full for the past four months, I still felt disconnected. I still felt like I didn't have a tribe. So—even though Camp Grounded was the most expensive thing I'd ever purchased besides rent—I decided to make an investment in myself. I needed to do something to alleviate the pain of not belonging and not feeling comfortable in my own skin.

Of course, as sure as I was, I was still nervous.

What if no one liked me?

What if I didn't fit in?

What if I wanted to leave but couldn't?

On June 10, sitting on a yellow school bus filled with complete strangers, I was about to find out.

A group of people onboard were wearing handmade name tags that announced their "camp name," AKA their nickname for the weekend.

Like Burning Man, Camp Grounded asks every participant to choose a new identity. It can be silly, like Hot Mess, Rumble the Lemur, or Yes And. The name can also be whimsical, like Bluejay, Cedar, or Prow Prow.

Sitting next to me was another camp newbie—Starlight. "What's your name?" she asked, giving me a nervous smile. "Jillian," I told her—then realized what she meant. Adjusting in my sticky plastic seat, I corrected myself. "Sorry," I laughed. "I've never done this before. My camp name is Lady. I chose it for literally one reason: I think someone saying, 'Hey, lady!' is funny."

Suddenly, a few people behind me burst into a chorus of "Lady" by Kenny Rogers. I grinned at Starlight, and we both joined in. These people were having more fun than anyone I'd been around in a long time—and their excitement was contagious.

As the bus got closer to the camp, I felt some nervousness build in my body. My heart rate increased, my palms got sweaty, and I kept nervously scratching my hands. I had no idea what I was in for.

When the bus hit Cold Spring, New York, we slowed to a halt in front of a grove of trees. Camp alumni placed their fingers on their lips and let out a low "Shhhhh" as our group leader stood up in front of the driver.

I was immediately drawn to her. She held herself with the unassuming confidence of a woman who has done some deep work on herself. I would eventually find out that she was a meditation teacher and belonging researcher. Years after that I would ask her to teach a workshop at Groundshift, a summer camp for activists that I would co-create in the coming years. For now, all I knew was that something about this woman impressed me.

She looked at the bus with a smile on her face and tears in her eyes. "I want to tell you a story about why Camp Grounded is special to me," she said, her voice shaking a little bit. "On my first bus ride up as a camper, I started to get bored—so I decided to doodle in my notebook. Then, since I wanted to make new friends, I asked other people to add their own drawings. Soon we were playing a game, where everyone had to add on to each other's creations. By the time we rolled into camp, we had created a masterpiece."

The entire bus was silent as she continued. "When I got off the bus, this short guy with some serious mischief in his eyes came right up to me. He asked to see what was in my hands, so I showed him the drawing. He paused, took a long moment to absorb it, and then let out a yell. It scared the crap out of me, but he scooped me up in his arms and twirled me around in a circle while calling out, 'You've got it!'"

At this point, a few people on the bus chuckled knowingly. I heard someone say, "Fidget."

"That man," she echoed, "was Fidget Wigglesworth. He's one of the Felix family members who started Camp Grounded. He taught me how important play is and created a space where I could explore that side of myself. He taught me that camp is about giving myself permission to act like a kid again."

She took a breath. "Fidget isn't here this year because he has cancer."

It was only a moment, but I felt those words hit my heart. I was surprised by how much that phrase—"he has cancer"—impacted me. After all, I'd never met Fidget before. Yet I could sense how important he was to some of the people on that bus. And I knew if it wasn't for him, I wouldn't have the opportunity to experience this magical weekend.

"We're about to enter camp," she said, gesturing to the trees around us. "So let's take a moment to leave that other world—of phones, and work, and distraction—behind. Let's breathe in being present, and playful, and here for each other."

She paused as the entire bus sat with their eyes closed, breathing deeply. After a few moments, she tapped the bus driver on the shoulder and he drove on. We twisted and turned through winding dirt roads, the stillness of the forest slowly making way to the sounds of people yelling and singing.

Her words rang in my mind: "Present, and playful, and here for each other."

And that's when I saw it—an entire parking lot filled with smiling, singing Camp Grounded staff. They were waving at the bus with huge grins on their faces, dancing, laughing, and blowing bubbles. They genuinely looked like they couldn't be more excited to see us. Again, my heart expanded like a balloon was filling up in my chest. These people were pure *joy.* I hadn't even talked to them yet, but I knew they were about to become my friends.

After I'd unloaded my bags, I was met with a pleasant surprise—cookies and milk. The tray, filled with gluten-free and vegan options, as well as cartons of "almond beverage," made me smile. The message of the small gesture was clear: "Everyone is welcome here."

Once I finished my snack, I was unexpectedly greeted by a woman in a hazmat suit. Disregarding my confused face, she took my hand and led me to a wall with a hole in it. After a few moments, a gloved hand popped out, scared the crap out of me, and grabbed my iPhone. After a small "Thank you!" came from behind the wall, the technology disappeared. I would not see it for the next three days.

Finally, I was guided by another mysterious hazmat-ed human to watch a fake educational video about the dangers of technology. To be honest, I don't remember the details. I was more focused on the feeling in my head of, "What the hell am I doing here?"

There's a photo of me from this moment that the Camp Grounded photographer, Troubador, took. I'm sitting next to Yes And, a woman who years later would let me sleep at her apartment in California when I spoke at a tech conference about creating spaces for connection. We would also share long sunset walks by Brooklyn Bridge Park while we ate ice cream and talked about our dating lives. We'd even spend a (platonic) Valentine's Day together at a very San Francisco cuddle party. Yet back at Camp Grounded, all I knew was that this woman seemed nice—and just as baffled as I was.

Finally, once we were fully initiated from the video, we were guided through a doorway and into a giant green field. People were already playing a game where you stick a loop of tape on your nose, face off against a stranger, and see who can emerge from the battle with two pieces on their snoot. Yes And and I immediately joined in. I laughed until I had cramps.

That was the start of an unforgettable weekend filled with honest conversations with former strangers, singing at the top of my lungs around a campfire, and getting more hugs than I'd ever had in my entire life. Over those four days, I was exposed to a level of openness and love that I didn't even know was possible. Suddenly, I didn't feel disconnected anymore. I felt seen. I felt like I belonged.

There was something sacred about my time at Camp Grounded. We had shared values of playfulness, openness, and vulnerageousness. (That's camp lingo for vulnerable and courageous.) People dropped their walls and shared their souls with each other. We participated in Camp Grounded ritual and had counselors who stepped into leadership after being campers themselves.

In other words, Camp Grounded is the perfect example of what I now call a healthy congregation. Yet at the time, all I knew was that I felt like I was home.

* * *

Once I returned to my twin bed in New York City, I was worried I'd fall out of touch with my new friends. After all, I'd been to plenty of events where I enjoyed the people I met, only to cease contact once the responsibilities of "real life" kicked back in. Yet to my delight, all of the New York campers wanted to stick together just as much as I did.

One week later, we were already having our first reunion at a bar in Brooklyn. The moment I walked in, I was greeted by Yes And, who asked me to put my phone in a basket. "Nice costume!" called out Bounce, referring to my dress and lipstick. She was right—she'd only seen me rocking my yoga pants and a bare face a week prior. I grinned and tried to make up for it by asking strangers in the bar if they'd like Mischief to paint their faces.

Cut to a few hours later, and we were attempting—admittedly unsuccessfully—to get the entire bar to do the wave with us.

It's now two and a half years after my first Camp Grounded experience, and those people are still in my life. A group of us showed up to cheer Smiley on at his book launch, and yelled "You're awesome!" when he finished his presentation. Rumble once had a concert in his backyard, which featured Prow Prow and Prospex—a couple who met at Camp Grounded—plus their newborn baby.

Eventually, the crew started to mingle with my other friends, as well. This led to one moment where my punk singer friend, Annie, turned to me and said, "This is the happiest group of people I have ever met." She went on to attend Camp Grounded herself, and now goes by Bambi.

While my Camp Grounded friends gather less frequently now, we still see each other a few times a year. In fact, I'm typing this exact sentence at a coworking day run by two friends from that first weekend.

Camp Grounded was a healthy congregation that transformed my life. It exposed me to a level of joy and community in adulthood that I didn't know was possible. That's why I was devastated when, in 2017, Levi—one of the Camp Grounded founders—died.

It was the first time I mourned someone I had never met.

When I got the news, I sat in my bedroom and wept, thinking about all the magic this thirty-two-year-old man would never get to create. I thought about his brother, Zev, who I loved dearly and felt a deep desire to hold in that moment. I thought about his entire family, who all worked together to make Camp Grounded happen while they also cared for Levi.

"It's not fair," I kept thinking. "It's not fair."

A few days later I went to Levi's memorial in New York City, hosted at a fellow camper's apartment. At first, I felt self-conscious about being there. After all, I'd never met Levi. Here were all these people who had danced with him, created with him, and been impacted by his mission to make the world a little more connected. I was afraid to admit that we'd never interacted. I also wondered if anyone there shared in my experience.

At one point in the night, my curiosity became too much. I asked people to raise their hand if they'd never met Levi. To my surprise, around a *third* of the room lifted their arms. And that's when it hit me. All around the country, from North Carolina to Texas to California, people weren't just gathering to remember Levi the man. They were also gathering to remember the camp and how that experience changed their lives.

Looking back, I realize how inevitable it was that Camp Grounded would become an important part of attendees' lives. After all, healthy congregations like it are rare and deeply needed. They alleviate the sense of loneliness most people walk around with every day. It makes sense that this community was a transformative experience that so many people—myself included—still hold close to their hearts.

I was mourning Levi because he dreamed of a different world, and I was lucky enough to have that creation be one of my first experiences of adulthood. Because of that weekend, I never doubted that I could live fiercely, passionately, and freely as an adult. That has been one of the biggest gifts of my life so far.

Camp Grounded gave me permission to be open and vulnerable with strangers. It encouraged me to own my mistakes and yell, "I'm awesome!" when I fuck up. It gently encouraged me to start to move away from the deeply engrained idea that I am defined by my job—and to stop judging others in the same way. It helped me put my preconceptions about age on pause and step into friendship with people who were in totally different stages of life. Camp

Grounded encouraged me to show up as my full, messy self—and taught me the power of congregation.

* * *

When I returned from Camp Grounded, I desperately wanted to find spaces that gave me the same feeling of connection. Now that I knew that feeling was possible, I wanted it all the time. So I turned my obsession with finding new events and tweaked it slightly. This time around, I knew I wanted to find healthy congregations.

Slowly, I started finding spaces that had a sense of kindness and community. These gatherings changed my life, and I owe the people who created them everything. Because event organizers don't get enough credit—both monetarily and in terms of gratitude—I want to express my thanks to Casey Rosengren and Leo Widrich from Balanced NYC, Jesse Israel and Lauren Bille from Medi Club, Juvoni Beckford and the Personal Development Nerds board, and Tasha Blank and The Get Down crew. You all created alternative realities that allowed me to step into a better version of myself and meet people I deeply love. Because of your vision, I found the congregation I didn't even know that I was hungry for. When I found them, I realized that I was starving.

At this moment in my life, I felt like I was in a love bubble. For the first time, I had deep friendships and consistent communities I could tap into for support. I would constantly say, with no trace of irony in my voice, "People are amazing."

And then something changed. Trump was elected.

I'll never forget what it felt like to watch our orange-skinned president get nominated on live TV. One of my roommates cried so hard I had to get up and hold her. On the adjacent couch, some visiting Canadians awkwardly stared off into the distance, unsure of what to say. In that moment, I was filled with rage. I started to question whether my faith in humanity was naive. Were we really just destined to fight against each other? Was I lying to myself when I believed people could hold each other with love?

After Trump's election, it felt like everyone in New York City was in a collective mourning period. No one made eye contact, and more people than usual were crying on public transportation. All around me, I heard people saying things like, "How can I trust anyone? My family voted for Trump!" "Some of my friends voted for him! Everyone is garbage." "This country is on fire. I'm just going to move."

But here's the thing. Even with a narcissistic orange running the country, I still had my healthy congregations to turn to.

On Tuesdays I could go and have a long conversation with my meditation friends. On Wednesday I could vent about the freelance struggle with my Personal Development Nerds. On Thursday I could cover myself in glitter and go dance with The Get Down crew. For me, the election didn't make me question my faith in humanity at large. Some people? Yes. But everyone on the planet? Definitely not.

In other words, I realized that so many New Yorkers were upset about the election because they didn't have places of support they could turn to and realize that people still cared about them.

So, like many others after the 2016 election, I started a project. It was called The Joy List.

The Joy List is a weekly newsletter of events that New Yorkers can attend by themselves and leave with a new friend. Unlike other events newsletters, every gathering we feature has a facilitated moment of connection. This means that a skilled facilitator will be there to help people drop their walls and connect in a way that's more meaningful than the standard small talk. Our mission is to make New York City, and eventually the world, a less lonely place.

Ironically, when I started The Joy List I genuinely thought I was part of a small percentage of people who felt deeply alone.

So, when I wrote about my experience with disconnection in my first newsletter, it felt like an extremely vulnerable share. At the time, I thought my words would only help a few people. Little did I know how many Americans loneliness actually touches.

Cut to a few weeks later, and word starts to get around that I'm "the loneliness woman." People I barely knew were coming up to me at parties and sharing their big secret. They don't feel like they belong. Folks from around the country found my email and started sharing their personal narratives around loneliness. These are a few of the messages I received:

"Since becoming a parent, I feel lonelier. I don't have as many meaningful, adult interactions, and I find myself wishing I had more close friendships. As an attorney and a parent of a 4- and 6-year old, the great majority of my time is devoted to work and family, and I'm not good at filling the rest of the time with developing meaningful social connections. Also as a secular humanist, I wish I had a secular 'church' and community I could belong to and meet on a weekly basis."

"I work from home so it is very isolating socially, and I noticed once you move beyond the college-aged bar crowds, things become hit or miss as far as reoccurring social connections. My interactions tend to be single servings, so I'm looking for a recurring environment."

"Despite having a lot of friends my whole life, I've felt lonely more often than I've felt not lonely. I think a big piece of that has been my fear of being vulnerable with the people close to me. I've been working on that in the last few years, but it's an ongoing process."

At this point, I had a pivotal realization. Loneliness is extremely common. People are just too ashamed to talk about it.

GETTING REAL ABOUT MY EXPERIENCE WITH LONELINESS

As I was researching for this book, I found a TED talk called "The Simple Cure for Loneliness."[7] In it, web show host Baya Voce explains how she incorporated ritual into her relationships to form more meaningful connections. At first glance, I thought it was pretty good advice. Then I scrolled down. These are some of the most up-voted comments, which I've edited for brevity:

"This talk made me so angry I want to smash my laptop against the wall. Oh so the cure for loneliness is to spend one night a week with my four close friends who I don't have? ... I bet she has no idea what it's like to finish her work week and know that she probably won't speak to another person face to face until she is back in work the next week."

"I found this video made me feel so much worse about my loneliness. She has no idea what she is talking about. What loneliness truly is and feels like... Not everyone has a significant other and family members. Honestly all this video has done for me is look at how pathetic my life is."

"How do you continue to feel good about yourself when you know you are a priority to NO ONE! ... I don't even have anyone to BURY me! If we had these people in our lives, we wouldn't BE lonely."

I felt the anger of these commenters in my bones. I felt their pain. They were expecting someone to get raw with them. They wanted to hear from someone who also struggled with feeling completely pointless in this world. Instead, they left feeling even more alone than before.

In the spirit of honesty, I'll let you know right now I have never had a moment in my life where I had zero connections. I have always had some sort of social support. Yet at the same time, I have also felt completely disconnected from others for over two decades. Even though people were all around me, I felt completely unsupported. I assumed no one could understand me. That was largely because I never opened up, and I didn't have a relationship with myself.

Because I want to model the vulnerability I want to see in the world, I'm going to dive into my own experience with loneliness throughout this book. While these stories don't make me look good, I hope they will normalize the lengths people will go to in order to feel connected.

After doing a lot of research, and having plenty of conversations, I've found that loneliness is not just an individual problem. It's a systemic issue with roots that grow in multiple directions.

David T. Hsu, a social scientist who wrote an amazing report about the loneliness epidemic, "Untethered," breaks down the problem into sixteen key categories.[8] As you look at this list, think about how many of these factors apply to you:

1. *Major changes in one's role (e.g., becoming a caregiver).*
2. *Certain occupations that tend to exacerbate isolation.*
3. *Current or past incarceration.*
4. *Growing older.*
5. *Identified with a group that faces discrimination.*
6. *Having a long commute.*
7. *Not participating in religious, civic, social, or shared interest groups.*
8. *Lower income.*
9. *Major changes in one's social circle (e.g., loss of a spouse, partner, or friend).*

10. *Living in a home or neighborhood that is geographically distant.*
11. *Certain mental or physical health disabilities.*
12. *Living alone.*
13. *Language or cultural barriers.*
14. *How and how much time one spends on smartphones, social media, and other media.*
15. *Lacking access to neutral public spaces (e.g., parks, sidewalks, plazas, cafes).*
16. *Having limited mobility.*

Seeing all of these loneliness qualifiers made me realize how I'm surrounded by, and immersed in, a culture of disconnection.

Many of these contributing factors are a daily part of my life and those of almost everyone around me. For example, I work for myself and often work from home alone. I spend hours on my computer, and most moments away are shared with my phone. I'm not a member of any religion, and as a New Yorker I have very limited access to green space. I can go weeks without getting into nature.

I own that as a straight, white, cisgender, upperclass, able-bodied, English-speaking, college-educated woman, I've got all the privilege in the world. Yet even I have a myriad of reasons why loneliness can be a regular part of my everyday experience.

While this book will focus on the power of healthy congregation to reduce feelings of isolation, I will also touch on a few other reasons why disconnection runs so deep in America. My hope is that you will judge yourself less for these feelings as your understanding of this phenomenon grows. After all, it's not your fault—our society is structured for loneliness. Of course people are unhappy.

KEY TAKEAWAYS

- People frequently need permission to be vulnerable and open up to strangers. Once permission is granted, magic happens.
- You might not realize that people around you are lonely, but that's just because you haven't opened up the conversation. If you share your own experience with feelings of disconnection, others will follow your lead.
- Loneliness is not just an individual problem. It is a systemic issue.

QUESTIONS TO CONSIDER

- What healthy congregations have you been a part of? Why did this gathering feel so powerful?

- What solutions can we co-create to address each of Hsu's sixteen reasons for loneliness?
- How can we reduce the shame of talking about loneliness and create spaces for people to talk about their feelings of disconnection?

2

GETTING FRIENTIMATE

"Some people go to priests, others to poetry, I to my friends."

—VIRGINIA WOOLF

Most people don't realize how crucial friendships are to our health.

I recently spoke at a conference in Baltimore about the importance of self-care. At the end of the day, I got to facilitate a conversation for ten of the attendees. My job was to encourage the women to talk about the new ways they decided to invest in themselves.

Being the group leader, I started by talking a little bit about my background. "Hi, I'm Jillian," I began. "I'm obsessed with loneliness. For that reason, I'm the founder of The Joy List, a weekly newsletter of events you can go to by yourself and leave with a new friend. Our mission is to make the world a less lonely place. I'm also writing a book, called *Unlonely Planet*, which has the same goal."

By this point, the circle of women had gotten quiet. I began to worry that I'd made them uncomfortable by dropping the L-word so many times. Nevertheless, after a pause, I awkwardly continued:

"So! In the spirit of community and accountability, I'd love for everyone to say their name and something they realized they need help with today."

Since many of the conference attendees were entrepreneurs, I expected the women to ask for assistance with their career. Yet my comments about disconnection seemed to jostle something loose inside them. Before I knew it, these women were leaning in and sharing from the heart.

It was magic.

Half of the group—women from multiple races and ability levels, ranging from their twenties to their sixties—said they needed help making friends. They also confessed that they had *never* admitted that to anyone else. Not even their spouse.

Here are some quotes from my group's conversation:

"I'm a huge extrovert. I have a ton of friends. No one understands when I say that I'm lonely. In fact, they tell me that I'm not grateful. But I don't have deep, consistent relationships. And I think that's partially because of shame. I worry that if people actually get to know the real me, they'll stop hanging out with me because they don't like what they see. Because if I'm being honest, I don't like what I see."

"I never felt lonelier than when I was in bed with my ex-husband. Now my kids have left the nest, and it's so hard for me to get out of the house and meet other people."

"I never had permission to say that I was lonely growing up. But I am. In fact, I started volunteering to help lonely people—just because I thought it would help me help myself. I even get massages because I haven't been touched by another person in over a year."

"I showed up today because I saw there was going to be a conversation around loneliness. I'm chronically ill, and it's hard for me to get out of bed. But I'm here because I know I need to talk about how lonely I am. That's why I showed up."

What hit me the hardest was the story of two women who were empty nesters—AKA their children had recently left for college. They were friends and had arrived together, yet were both still craving connection. They each told me they were afraid to reach out to the other woman.

"I don't invite her over because I worry about being a bother," one of the women admitted. "I worry the drive will take too long. I worry she won't be able to find a parking meter. I worry I'm wasting her time."

She paused, looking between me and her friend. There were tears in her eyes. "Now that I say it out loud, I feel silly."

Can you imagine? These women were all walking around, carrying the shame of their loneliness. Little did they know that the average American only has one friend, and 75 percent of people are not satisfied with their friendships. This group was anything but alone in their experience, but they needed the opportunity to share to realize it.

These small moments reveal a much larger problem within the conversation about loneliness—our shame of even speaking about it in the first place. It's a true double bind. We feel too embarrassed to talk about our isolation, yet the issue itself would hold less stigma if it was discussed more often. This shame spiral prevents us from being in congregation with each other. We assume no one else wants to connect, when in reality, most people are dying for someone to reach out.

JUNK VALUES

I originally stumbled across the phrase "junk values" in researcher Johann Hari's book, *Lost Connections*.[9] He explains, based off the work of social scientist, professor Tim Kasser, that people have two types of motivation: intrinsic and extrinsic. When we do something simply because it brings us joy, we are intrinsically motivated.

When we do something for someone else—to get them to pay us, sleep with us, or think we're successful—that's extrinsic motivation. And as it turns out, people who do things for extrinsic reasons are far less happy than people who operate based on their own internal compass. As Hari says in the book, twenty-two different studies have found that the more materialistic and extrinsically motivated someone is, the more depressed they will be. In addition, twelve found that looking outward for satisfaction results in increased anxiety.

As someone who can rely on others for feelings of well-being, these stats rocked me.

Hari explained the concept of junk values in an article for *Los Angeles Times*: "Junk food looks like food, but it doesn't meet our underlying nutritional needs. In a similar way, junk values don't meet our underlying psychological needs—to have meaning and connection in our lives. Extrinsic values are KFC for the soul. Yet our culture constantly pushes us to live extrinsically."[10]

"Junk values" feels like the perfect two-word explanation for why I—and so many people around me—struggle with feeling discontent. We focus on things that don't make us truly happy and toss aside the aspects of living that fill us up. One perfect example is the belief that committed friendships are a luxury, rather than a necessity.

As I started to do research on this topic, I stumbled upon *Tribe*, a fascinating book about belonging by author and filmmaker, Sebastian Junger.[11] He does a great job of explaining why relying on ourselves alone, rather than our community, is detrimental to our mental health. According to a global survey by the World Health Organization, people in wealthy countries suffer from depression as much as eight times the rate they do in poor countries.[12] People in countries with large income disparities—like the United States—run a much higher lifelong risk of developing severe mood disorders.

As Junger explains, "The mechanism seems simple: poor people are forced to share their time and resources more than wealthy people are, and as a result live in closer communities. Inter-reliant poverty comes with its own stresses—and certainly isn't the American ideal—but it's much closer to our evolutionary heritage than affluence."

In America, we value independence and the ability to take care of ourselves. As a result, we miss the richness and beauty of forging deeper connections with our neighbors. By ignoring what is truly important, we damage our mental health.

THE FRIENDSHIP GAP

Shasta Nelson understands this misalignment well. She also wins the award for best job title ever—friendship expert.

Yet that wasn't always her role. She used to be a pastor. For an entire decade, Shasta did the works: giving sermons, meeting with her parishioners, and training small group leaders. And then, as she began to see the need for community all around her, she became just as excited about creating belonging outside of the church as she was within it.

Shasta originally became a member of the clergy because she was interested in relationships. "I was inspired by the idea of a place where people came together to try and improve their lives," Shasta told me. "One of my favorite things about pastoring was consistently seeing the same people and getting to be a part of their personal growth."

The problem? Just because churches want to be a community for people doesn't mean it happens automatically. Attending church services isn't enough to leave us feeling seen. For example, a woman once entered Shasta's office, visibly angry. Without taking a breath, she announced: "I'm leaving the church." Shasta was understandably shocked. She had no idea what prompted this sudden change. It turns out, the woman had recently had a miscarriage, and was upset that no one had noticed that she hadn't been at church in two weeks.

"The strange thing?" Shasta said. "No one even knew this woman was pregnant. How would they know to ask? But that's when I realized—she really just needed somewhere to share. She needed a place for her life experience to be honored and validated." Churches, like everywhere, have to intentionally foster what Shasta calls Frientimacy: allowing people to feel seen in a safe and satisfying way.

This issue, combined with Shasta's passion for helping people, led to the development of a side hustle—being a life coach for women. Little did she know that her new clients would help her clarify her true mission.

"I was living in San Francisco at the time," Shasta told me. "I was lying in bed, wide awake. It was the middle of the night and I couldn't sleep."

She kept thinking about one of her clients—a lawyer. "She was one of the most ambitious, impressive women I knew," Shasta said.

Originally, the lawyer had asked for coaching because she was stressed about a career transition. Yet one day, Shasta asked about who was supporting her.

"I asked, 'What are your friends saying about this decision in your life?'" Shasta said. "And she told me she'd lost touch with them."

After she said this, Shasta paused for a moment.

"I'll need to be careful with how I say this because I do appreciate the coaching industry," she said. "But much of what a really good life coach does is what an amazing friend could do for you. They help you feel seen, reflect back what they're hearing, encourage you to trust yourself, and ask good questions. That lawyer? Nobody was there to support her except for a life coach she hired."

Yet the lawyer's predicament wasn't what kept Shasta up in the middle of the night. In reality, she was upset because she'd heard *three* other women tell her the exact same thing that week. Their friendships were up in the air, and they had no idea where to find a support system.

Of course, Shasta wanted to help them find connection. "We used to rely on bowling leagues, civic clubs, and churches to be our go-to places for community. But that doesn't work anymore," Shasta said. "Besides, belonging is more than just knowing where to meet people." Even as a former pastor, Shasta acknowledged that church isn't the automatic answer for developing community.

"Quite honestly, a lot of people walk into church and feel like it's cliquish," Shasta admitted. "So I can't just tell her to walk in on Sunday! Even if she went, it's not a guaranteed fit. For many people, the church is not a safe place to be vulnerable and show up with your most honest self."

The next morning, Shasta woke up, made herself some coffee, and decided she was going to build a website to help women make new friends. "I was much less passionate about getting people to believe something in a religious context and more excited about their personal growth, their relationship health, and who they were becoming," Shasta told me. "People think that just by attending church, they're a part of the community. But really, our relationship expectations can only go as high as we practice."

A few months later, Shasta had officially left the church and started GirlFriendCircles.com, a free community that introduces women to each other and inspires friendship.

Shasta was going from the safety and predictability of her church life into the great unknown. She knew plenty of people who were pastors—and absolutely no one who identified as a "community builder." Nevertheless, she decided to be a pioneer and teach others how to create deeper relationships. "If I left the church, I knew somebody else would take my place," Shasta said. "But if I didn't go out and create connection and community? Not many other people would fill that gap right away."

Shasta started her journey simply—by introducing women to each other. She was essentially a friendship matchmaker. "Yet quickly, it became incredibly clear what the real problem was," Shasta said. "In reality, the issue is not that we don't know how to meet people. Most of us meet new people on a regular basis! The real problem is that we don't know how to actually 'date' people. We don't know how to turn those relationships into close friendships. We're not lonely due to lack of interaction, but rather because of a lack of intimacy."

Shasta grinned. "When I had that realization? That's when I got super passionate and never looked back."

While Shasta has since written two books on friendship and now gives keynotes on how to build healthier relationships, she still has a heart for the role that churches can play in building community. Fortunately, a lot of congregations are excited to learn how they can strengthen the relationships between their members.

Recently, Shasta worked with a mega church that was having an unusual problem—people in their small groups were diving into intimate conversation too quickly. "They had been working off the premise that the quicker we're vulnerable, the more we bond," Shasta said. "But that can lead to two or three people taking too much of the group's time and bringing down the joy for the rest. Being needy is not going to create true community."

Shasta taught the church's leaders that a true community needs to build up intimacy slowly. "They were literally starting the group by asking people to share about the hardest thing that was going on in their lives," Shasta said. "And strangers were talking about death and disaster. It was just too heavy."

Now, the group is run a little differently. The pastor opens with the questions: "What in your life is bringing you joy right now? What's one thing that's more stressful?" As a result, the conversation is more upbeat. In addition, everyone has an equal opportunity to share. Shasta slowly adjusts the questions to be increasingly vulnerable as the group gets more comfortable with each other. This ensures the parishioners leave the group feeling seen and safe. As a result, they're more likely to attend the following week.

"Sure, there are those magical moments when we have a conversation with somebody on an airplane or on a retreat who we will never see again, and we're really open and honest," Shasta said. "But if people want to have a friendship, they need to do that repetitively."

FINDING FRIENTIMACY

In 2017, Shasta gave a TED talk called "Frientimacy: The 3 Requirements of All Healthy Friendships." She kicks it off by making this bold statement: "I am worried about the vast majority of us in this room who are lonely and don't acknowledge it."[13]

We live in an era when our social networks are bigger than ever—yet we also report feeling more disconnected and less understood. Why? As Shasta explains, "Modern loneliness is not because we need to know more people. It's because we need to be more known by a few. We're emotionally lonely."

One of the times Shasta felt the loneliest was, in fact, when she was with five of her friends. It had been a month since they'd last seen each other, so they sat in a circle to discuss what had happened in the past thirty-one days. Shasta shared,

"When it got to the fourth person, she said something that reminded somebody of something they had read, which reminded that person of something their sister had said over the holiday. You know where this is going. The train left the station. And I had not shared!"

She sat there, waiting for someone to notice that her turn had been skipped. But before Shasta knew it, everyone looked at their watch and realized that it was time to leave. Shasta left the gathering feeling hurt. "My loneliness wasn't from lack of friendships," Shasta said. "My loneliness was because I didn't feel seen."

This insight led Shasta to dive into research about the state of friendship. She asked over six thousand people how, on a scale of one to ten, they would rate the closeness of their friendships. The results were bleak. Up to 70 percent of us rate a five or below. In fact, we are two to four times more likely to put a one or a two than we are to say we're fulfilled with a nine or a ten.

Ouch.

Yet this skill can be learned. Shasta herself is the perfect example. When I got on the phone to interview her, I asked about a recent moment when she felt like she truly belonged. Without a second thought, she told me a story—about the same group of five friends—that is the polar opposite of the anecdote from her TED Talk.

"We hopped on a video call and started sharing the things that made the biggest impact on us since we had last seen each other," Shasta recalled. Now they have a sharing structure, which ensures that everyone feels seen. Each woman shares the hardest thing going on in her life, as well as the biggest wins. "It's amazing to me how we can step into intimacy like that on Skype," Shasta said. "But it's because we've done the work, and we have that consistency."

I asked Shasta for some actionable strategies people can use to create more meaningful friendships. Being a researcher, she didn't let me down. These are the three relationship-strengthening tactics she shared:

1) In order to feel seen we have to practice *vulnerability* (the sharing of who we are).

2) In order for it to feel satisfied we have to practice *positivity* (the reward and enjoyment of each other).

3) In order for it to feel safe, we have to practice *consistency* (the regularity of interaction and behavior).

According to Shasta, every healthy friendship has to practice those three requirements.

Yet if friendship is so important, why do we talk about those relationships so infrequently... while romantic love is the center of almost every conversation, TV show, movie, and book? (Fun fact: romance accounts for a third of the US fiction market.)[14]

Arizona State philosopher, Elizabeth Brake, coined a term that summarizes our culture-wide obsession with romantic and sexual love: *amatonormativity.* As she says in her book, *Minimizing Marriage: Marriage, Morality, and the Law*, the word refers to "the assumptions that a central, exclusive, amorous relationship is normal for humans, in that it is a universally shared goal, and that such a relationship is normative, in that it should be aimed at in preference to other relationship types."[15]

In other words, we treat romance like it should always be aspired to and that it is the best type of relationship. Yet this obsessive focus on partnership is damaging to people's sense of community. Relying on one person to provide everything for us is an unhealthy expectation. It keeps us from connecting with our neighbors and forging intimate friendships.

In an article titled "How to Stay Married," Stephanie Coontz, author of several sociology publications, argues that social ties outside of a marriage can ease emotional pressure and create stronger relationships overall.[16] She cites a study by sociologists Naomi Gerstel and Natalia Sarkisian, which found that married people are 40 percent less likely to socialize with friends than those who are not married. In addition, married people are less likely to offer emotional support to friends and neighbors.[17] I think this is less a condemnation of marriage overall, but rather a commentary on how our culture insists that a married couple only needs each other. In reality, everyone needs a network of support.

Our cultural obsession with romantic love, and complete lack of attention given to friendship, is a perfect example of our "junk values." What if we dedicated one quarter of the time that we spend talking about finding a partner—or, let's be real, casual hookup—to how we can become better friends to each other?

What if our longing for a partner was actually a simple desire to be seen and held?

TOGETHERNESS THROUGH TOUCH

A friend once sent me a tweet that highlights this point perfectly. As of this writing, it has 115,994 retweets and

468,425 likes. The message, from a user named "hummus" on Twitter, was this:

"Does anyone else feel 'touch deprived'? & I'm not talking about touching in a sexual way but simple platonic gestures like hugs, having someone play with your hair, resting your head on someone's shoulder and so on...no one prepared me for how lonely adult-friendships really are."[18]

If you're looking for more data to prove that the way we operate in relationship is broken, this is it.

Over a hundred thousand people resonated with this message enough to publicly share it on their own Twitter page. Almost half a million hit "like." Clearly, a large percentage of people feel like the way they're approaching friendship is failing. But why?

One big part of the equation that's missing is platonic touch.

When I moved to NYC, I was severely touch deprived. I didn't have a romantic partner or close friends who I was comfortable snuggling with. I didn't even have the self-knowledge to ask, "Hey, can you give me a long hug? I haven't gotten enough cuddles today."

Is it hard for you to imagine saying that? For a long time, it was for me, too. Admitting that I need touch felt desperate and needy. Thankfully, understanding the positive benefits of platonic touch has helped me shift my perspective. Besides, being "needy" has a bad rap. If you put a positive spin on it, it means you know what you want, and you ask for it. That's empowered as hell.

According to a paper published in *PLOS One,* hugs can have a measurable impact on mood and stress after social conflict. A simple squeeze can increase positive feelings and reduce negative ones on days when people experienced relationship problems.[19]

As an article in Psychology Spot explained, a hug stimulates the production of dopamine—AKA the "pleasure hormone." It also increases the production of oxytocin, which is known as the "love hormone." Dopamine relieves stress while oxytocin allows us to emotionally connect with and trust others. That's a pretty good combo, right?

In addition, a study conducted at the Advanced Telecommunications Research Institute International in Kyoto found that a hug or loving caress can affect the brain's ability to imagine the body. This means that physical contact is essential to develop and maintain a healthy body image.

Last but not least, a different study conducted at the University College London found that this type of body contact offers pleasant tactile sensations, which generate a series of "proprioceptive signals." These signals help us feel ownership of our body and know we are worthy of love.[20]

As someone who is a recovering anorexic and binge eater, this research made complete sense to me. When I was engaging in self-harming behavior, I didn't want people to touch me. Binging gave me an excuse to keep everyone at arm's length. I felt disgusting, which was the perfect excuse to keep people out. Yet even when I was "thin enough" to be intimate with someone, I couldn't stay present with them. I disassociated from my body.

I deeply relate to what emotional eating expert, Geneen Roth, says in her book *When Food Is Love:* "When I allow myself to be thin, I told myself, it will be symbolic of my willingness to receive pleasure; being thin will be my statement to myself and the world that after so many years, I finally believe I am worthy of love." [21]

Of course, being thin does *not* mean that I was suddenly able to be intimate with someone. It didn't mean I could connect on an emotional level or acknowledge my needs either. Looking back at my college self, I can see that I wasn't hungry for casual sex. I was craving touch and intimacy.

Being a part of a healthy congregation, like a weekly cuddle puddle—AKA gathering for people who want their touch tank filled up—would have done wonders for me. I just never knew that was an option. If I had, perhaps I would have sought out connection in healthier ways, rather than desperately looking to casual sexual encounters for connection.

Now I know that one of my primary love languages—AKA the way I like to receive affection—is physical touch. (The others are receiving gifts, quality time, words of affirmation, and acts of service.) Since I understand this need, I can ask for what I want. This can look like putting my head on a friend's shoulder, asking for a long hug, or going to a massage workshop. I don't go swiping through Tinder like a mad woman now because I don't need that connection. I have other ways to get it.[22]

I saw how hungry people are for touch firsthand when I gave out hugs by the Union Square Farmers Market in New York City. Yep. I was one of *those people,* walking around the vegetable stands with a sign that said "Free hugs!" As I wandered, I called out, "Free range hugs! They're good for your health! Totally organic."

While some people were understandably hesitant to hug a stranger, I noticed they got more comfortable once someone else gave me a squeeze and I didn't try to rob them. Suddenly, slowly, I had a line of people waiting to hug me. One woman started crying and said that her boyfriend had just broken up with her. She took my sign for a while, and joined me in giving people hugs. Another man, a really big guy covered in tattoos, teared up after our embrace. "I really needed that," he said, looking a little embarrassed. "It's okay," I said reassuringly. "We all do."

RETREAT VERSUS REALITY

Living in New York City can be draining. An average day for me looks like: wake up at 7 a.m., do my morning routine, knock out some writing, take the subway to my gym in the East Village, work out, walk across the street to my coworking space, answer emails, have a meeting, do some more writing, take the subway back to Brooklyn, meet up with my roommates to eat dinner at home, walk to an event, experience the event, get some tea with friends after, walk home. Collapse.

While I'm blessed to have such a full life—and fully acknowledge that I've chosen to live this way—it wears on me. I miss nature and know I don't get enough of it. Being in such a high-energy city makes my body tense, and that—combined with my own perfectionism and intense desire to thrive in my work—results in a constant low-level buzz of anxiety. Despite my meditation, journaling, and regular deep talks with friends, that feeling is there. And it hurts.

That's why, when a friend offered me a free spot on his retreat upstate, I was ecstatic. I got to stay in a yurt in the middle of the woods? And eat home-cooked food? And do yoga? Sign. Me. Up.

Those three days were soul-filling. I was surrounded by New Yorkers who prioritized getting nature into their lives, had deep spiritual practices, and somehow knew the right plants to make into a tea. (That blew my mind.) They seemed comfortable and grounded in their bodies, which made me hyperaware of the fact that I wasn't.

Over the course of the weekend, we played silly improv games, shared our prayers around a campfire, and went on a silent hike to a waterfall. We did yoga every morning, danced until we were exhausted and sweaty, and shared plenty of long meals.

One of my favorite elements of the retreat was the two puppies wandering around. They were friends, and would frequently run off from the group to bark, chase each other in circles, and roll around in the grass. One chilly morning, slowly sipping my coffee, I started to tear up while watching them play. Those fluff balls represented a form of pure joy and freedom that I felt like I'd lost—and only started to get reacquainted with over the weekend.

During the last hours of the experience, we all gathered to share how we were feeling about returning to the "real world." Because of the safe space the facilitators had created throughout the weekend, I felt comfortable getting emotional. When my turn came to speak, tears started welling up in my eyes. At first, I couldn't understand why. So I took a moment to pause, breathe, and feel into my emotions. Finally, my thoughts landed on this:

"Why is this the retreat?" I said angrily. "Shouldn't regular life feel this good? Shouldn't we all have community dinners, and nature, and movement every day? It makes me sad that I'm leaving this."

Everyone in the circle nodded knowingly. It was true—multiple people had shared similar sentiments: "I hate that this is the escape. I want my life to have more of these elements. And I'm not sure how to get that."

Dave Adams, the Head Concierge of Ashram Galactica—a camp at Burning Man—felt something similar the first time he came back from the playa. (To break down some of those terms, Burning Man is a festival in the middle of the Nevada desert where seventy thousand people create, and then break down, a city called Black Rock. That land is also called the playa.)

Burning Man is known for being a space where people are incredibly open. Friendships—and romantic relationships—can be formed in moments. "Everyone is open to connection," Dave told me. "You meet someone and they are incredibly kind. Every interaction is elevated. It's magic."

Going from this environment back to New York City was a shock to Dave's system. "Everyone was on the subway with their headphones in, heads down, no one looking at each other," Dave said. "It was like I could walk around for the whole day without anyone making eye contact with me."

I've had similar experiences. I remember coming home from a silent meditation retreat and seeing the deep pain on the faces of people on the train. I wanted to talk with them and learn what was wrong. Yet my own discomfort with breaking the unspoken NYC rule of "stay in your space" prevented me from doing that. I felt the hurt of disconnection and loneliness, and I wondered if these people would have the chance to share a conversation that day. Considering the statistics about loneliness that I included earlier in the book, over half of them wouldn't. I wanted to cry.

In that moment, I recalled a quote from a meditation teacher, Larry Yang, in his book, *Awakening Together*: "As we become more mindful, we actually see even more suffering than we had previously noticed."

Now that I understand a hunger for connection is everywhere, I've arrived at a place where I can't ignore the pain anymore.

SEVEN STEPS TO CREATE CONNECTION

"My friend just moved to New York City. Can you help them find a community?"

Since I run The Joy List, people ask me this question all the time. While I *love* that they trust me to connect their friend to quality people, there's only so much time I can afford to give for free. Yet my people-pleasing nature led me to keep saying "yes," only to find myself feeling resentful later. I was experiencing the classic "connector burnout."

That's when my friend Jared suggested I experiment with offering my connecting as a service. "Call it something like, 'Find Your People,'" he said. "Talk to folks who recently moved here for thirty minutes, learn what they're struggling with, and then send them a custom calendar of people to meet and things to do."

I wasn't sure about the idea, so I threw it out to the newsletter. Would anyone be interested? A few dozen responses later, and it was clear the answer was a resounding yes.

Each thirty-minute call felt like a deep dive into one of the many reasons why we experience loneliness. I learned more about my audience than I ever could have anticipated—and was struck by how much of their lives people were willing to share. It didn't feel like a consulting call. It felt like a therapy session.

After hundreds of conversations with people about their experiences around loneliness, these are seven of the key lessons to keep in mind when finding your community in a new place:

1) Couples can be lonely, too: As you saw in the "Friendship Gap" section of this chapter, one relationship cannot fulfill your every need. That's why a rich network of friends is always necessary, regardless of having a romantic partner or not. Throughout my social calendar calls, I talked to multiple couples who were happy in their relationship yet felt the burden of their partner relying on them for everything.

"I want more consistency in my interactions with friends," one man told me. "I feel like I see them once every five weeks. I want a stronger sense of community."

2) Community is not catered to older folks: Anyone who's over fifty is more than welcome at the events I host and feature in The Joy List. Yet I'll admit, that person will be out of the average age range. I've had to tell curious Joy List-ers this before, and they inevitably feel disappointed that they're going to stick out.

Even communal housing options in New York City typically host people in their twenties and thirties. While an older person is welcome in this space, they won't necessarily fit in. Running The Joy List has taught me how few intergenerational events, and housing options, there are in New York. My guess is if that's the case here, it's also happening in other cities.

However, some do exist. Programs like DOROT give older folks the opportunity to mentor high schoolers. The students get help with their homework, and the mentors have a sense of purpose. In the end, both feel more connected. In a different realm, Nuns and Nones gives both women religious and millennials the opportunity to share their spiritual worldview. Both parties learn from each other and feel like their voice matters.

3) Finding your people is a commitment: I have chatted with so many people who desperately want closer friendships yet convince themselves they don't have the time to create those relationships.

"I don't even get out of the office," one woman told me. "But I don't feel lonely in the sense that the place makes me lonely. It's me. I'm not making the time to put myself out there."

Carlin Ross, a sex education teacher, once told me that women feel so much shame around their sexuality because they simply don't understand their bodies. "Yet having a great sex life doesn't come automatically," she told me. "People have to invest the time and energy to teach themselves. But we think we should already know everything. So we feel broken when our sex lives aren't fantastic."

That same concept applies to amazing friendships. They take a big investment, yet we're never explicitly told that. So, when we live without them, we live with the shameful assumption that something is wrong with us—rather than the understanding that we're simply not growing our skill set. How can anyone expect a friendship to grow if you don't know how to nurture it?

4) **Our homes can make us happy:** So many people in New York City are desperate for housing and choose to live with anyone who seems mildly sane. Yet if you have the luxury of choosing who you live with, why not share space with someone who makes you a better person?

Moving in with roommates who care about me, and make an active effort to help me grow, has improved my quality of life like nothing else. Don't assume you'll find great relationships outside of your apartment. You sleep and eat your meals there. You should have some friendship as well!

5) Don't consume, collaborate: It's easy to show up at an event and expect to be catered to. And sometimes that's nice. Yet it's often more rewarding to contribute to the space. This is why I always recommend that people volunteer at events. Not only will this save money, but it also allows them to meet the organizers and their fellow volunteers. You already have some shared values with those people, which means you're likely to get along.

Volunteering also helps with social anxiety. When new people enter the room, you don't have to stand there wondering what to do. You have a purpose—checking them in, serving food, taking their coat. This helps conversation move more naturally and gives you a sense of direction.

This rule applies for more informal gatherings, as well. You could just show up at someone's brunch and expect to be fed. But the hosts will appreciate you—and you'll feel more at ease—if you bring a bunch of ingredients to create a small dish like a fancy cheese plate. You have something to occupy your hands, a conversation starter, and instant gratitude from the hosts and guests right off the bat. Boom.

6) Find the connectors: Every community has someone who absolutely loves connecting people to each other. You'll recognize them by their insane amount of Facebook friends, a friendly grin, and the fact that at least three people have told you, "Wait, you haven't met (insert name here) yet? They know everyone!"

If you have social media, locating these people is easy—especially if you're about to move to a new city. Simply post something along the lines of:

"Hey everyone! I'm moving to Chicago and looking for connections to amazing people. Who should I meet?"

If you're searching for more connections in your current area, simply remove the "I'm moving to Chicago" section. You'll be surprised by how many people are tagged. Folks love to help. You just need to give them permission to do their thing.

7) Be a gatherer: New Yorkers love to say, "People are too busy. They won't come to an event if I invite them." I love you, but I'm going to call bullshit. SO many people are waiting to be invited. Even if they can't go, or are too anxious to attend, they will be so thankful that you thought of them and reached out. It's a gift to tell someone you'd like to spend time with them.

I think a lot of people are too passive in their social lives. And I get it. The fear of being rejected can prevent us from reaching out. Yet, I'm a firm believer in what Adam "Smiley" Poswolsky, a Camp Grounded counselor, said in a memorial piece to its founder on Medium: "Some people spend their time living, some people spend their time creating the world they actually want to live in." Which one do you want to be?[23]

KEY TAKEAWAYS

- Intimate friendships and platonic touch are crucial for our physical and mental health.
- Being extrinsically motivated and individually focused is a recipe for discontent and mental illness.
- Finding and maintaining meaningful friendships requires just as much of a commitment as maintaining a romantic partnership.

QUESTIONS TO CONSIDER

- How can we incorporate ritual into friendship as much as we do with romance? What is the friend equivalent of a marriage ceremony?
- What spaces can we create that allow for anyone to receive platonic touch?
- How can we make friendship counseling as accepted as couples counseling?

3

CREATING AN ALTERNATE UNIVERSE

"It is possible that the next Buddha will not take the form of an individual. The next Buddha may take the form of a community—a community practicing understanding and loving kindness, a community practicing mindful living. This may be the most important thing we can do for the survival of the earth."

—THICHT NHAT HANH

"You look pathetic."

These words were spat in my face by a blackout drunk man with a tie wrapped around his forehead. We were on the dance floor in a dark East Village bar, standing underneath the world's tiniest disco ball.

To be honest, I can't blame him. I *did* look pathetic. Everyone was dancing their faces off, and I was making things awkward by standing there, swaying painfully. My hands were sweaty, my heart was racing, and my body was screaming at me, "Get out of here, you idiot!"

Yet I was there with my friends, and they were somehow having a good time. So, I escaped in the most socially acceptable way possible. I fled to the bathroom. For the second time in thirty minutes.

If it's not already clear, I have a paralyzing fear of dancing. Or at least I used to.

Growing up, I never had good dance experiences. I took ballroom for two years and was given an ultimatum by my teachers: compete or quit. I joined one group competition and somehow ended up doing a turn that resulted in me standing in the middle of a circle... sans partner.

Later, I joined a hip-hop dance class. I was so bad that, when I asked my strict Irish mom if I could quit before the recital, she actually agreed.

Finally, in high school, I asked a boy to a school dance. He said yes, and I was elated... until the next day when he told me that he'd rather go with someone else.

Needless to say, I get anxious around dance floors.

After that incident in the bar, I promised myself I would get over my fear, no matter what. So, like any good millennial, I did some Googling. That's when I discovered a dance party called The Get Down.

I clicked on their website and was greeted with this message:

"It doesn't matter if you think you can dance. It doesn't matter what you wear, what you look like or who your friends are. Here's what we want to know: Are you willing to embrace your own sweat? Are you willing to groove harder than you have in years? Are you willing to make three hundred new best friends in three hours? If the answer is yes, then welcome to the family."

Woah.[24]

A few days later, I found myself standing outside of Cielo—a club in the Meatpacking District—at 6 p.m. I was wearing black workout pants and a plain blue tank top along with a confused expression. I had no idea if I was in the right place.

Thankfully, a petite woman standing by the door, rocking a hairdo that incorporated giant pink feathers, spotted me. I'd later find out that her name was Rachel, and she runs a sexual empowerment company called Heart-On. "Darling!" she exclaimed with a huge grin. "Are you here for The Get Down?" I nodded nervously, and some people in the line cheered. I stood behind a guy wearing khakis and a button up shirt. We started chatting and within a few minutes were at the front of the line.

"Have you been to The Get Down before?" Rachel asked when we arrived, leaning in with a catlike grin. "Nope!" me and Business Casual Man said in unison. Her smile got even bigger as she theatrically threw her arms up in the air and pronounced, "At The Get Down we practice enthusiastic consent!" Her energy was so intense that I actually took a step back. "Do you know what that means?" At this point, I'd been to enough hippie-esque parties that I knew how to respond. "Consent is sexy and mandatory!" I called back. "Correct!" Rachel cried and offered me a piece of dark chocolate to "open my heart chakra."

Thinking we were done, I held out my waiting ID to the bouncer. Rachel stopped me. "Two more rules!" she announced. "No phones on the dance floor and no drinks on the dance floor. Agreed?" I mustered up as much enthusiasm as I could, and shouted, "Agreed!" She paused, pleased with my loudness. And then, finally, she stepped aside to let us in the front door with one final, "Have fun, lovelies!"

But the party couldn't start just yet. We entered another line—coat check. All around me, people were removing layers. Shocked, I realized that my partner in crime was taking off his shirt.... and his khakis. Underneath his business veneer—like a superhero wearing a secret costume—he had on patterned leggings and a tiny tank top. A very muscular man behind me was wearing a yellow mesh shirt with nothing underneath, pineapple printed booty shorts, and bright pink sweatbands on his wrists and ankles. Suddenly, I felt like I was wearing the worst outfit possible.

Finally, I paid for my coat, gave my name to a man with a bright orange Mohawk, and passed through a curtain onto the dance floor. Only then did I realize I had made a horrible mistake.

I showed up early to a dance party. And I'm afraid of dancing.

Roughly fifteen people were in the space. They were moving so freely that I assumed they were on drugs. Only later did I learn that roughly 90 percent of the people at The Get Down are sober.

I sat awkwardly on a couch and watched a man slither across the floor on his belly. Slowly, he moved to a crouch, positioned himself on all fours, closed his eyes, and started bouncing up and down to the beat.

By this point, my entire body was in flight mode. It felt like I'd swallowed a ten-pound weight. My heart was racing, my hands were sweating, and my throat started to tense up.

In that moment, all I wanted to do was leave. But I stayed.

Two hours later, the floor was packed. Everyone was sweaty and smiling, eyes bright. The group stood in a tight, pulsating circle around a man who was playing the drums so hard he was red in the face. Every few seconds, someone would let out a tribal yell. I stayed to the side, too awkward to get into the center of the action.

Thankfully, a woman noticed me standing by myself. She smiled and put her arm around my shoulders, helping me move to the rhythm. Together we cheered for the musician, brought our bodies to the floor, and started using our hands to pound out the beat on the ground. Someone started chanting, "Yes!" I joined in.

Soon, the whole group was jumping up and down, arms around each other, yelling, "Yes!" in unison to the sounds of the drummer. I closed my eyes, noticed the sweat drip down my back, felt my heart beat hard in my chest, and smiled. I was actually having an enjoyable dance experience. Even more unbelievable, I felt *free*.

Suddenly, I noticed that the music had lowered. The entire room, as if on command, got still. "Everybody close your eyes," said a voice that seemingly came from nowhere. After looking around, I realized that it was coming from the party's DJ, Tasha Blank. Duh. Slightly elevated behind the DJ decks, she looked over the room regally. While her expression was calm, there was mischief in her eyes. In a moment, she had made a room that was screaming at the top of its lungs become completely quiet. She emanated a sort of loving power that I was completely intimidated yet simultaneously impressed by.

I looked around, unsure what to do. But, everyone actually *did* have their eyes closed. And so—a little bit uncomfortable—I followed suit.

"Breathe in," Tasha whispered into the microphone. "And breathe out." A long "Ahhhhh" echoed in every corner as over one hundred people exhaled.

I felt a shiver shoot from the top of my head to the tips of my toes as she purred her last words:

"Whatever you're feeling is perfect. Whatever you're being is perfect. Whatever you're thinking is perfect. You are right on time. You are exactly where you need to be. This is the moment when everything becomes possible."

The entire room was still, silent, breathing together.

And then—after what could have been thirty seconds or five minutes—she yelled, "So, are you ready to dance?"

With that, the room cheered. The music was back, and the drummer started up again. People threw up their arms, and I joined them. In that moment, I noticed I was dancing more freely than before. I was looking at other people less and losing myself to the music more.

Something had shifted.

I have a theory that people are loyal to the event that facilitates their transformation.

The Get Down is one of those spaces for me. After that party, I made sure I never missed one. It is marked in my Google Calendar, every other Thursday, until the end of time.

Fast forward two years, and I'm a promoter for the party. I feature it in my newsletter and invite anyone and everyone who I think will benefit from it. This includes Laura, David, and Duncan—three of my closest friends who all happened to be having a really shitty week at the same time. To fix the funk, I make a proposal. Let's dance our faces off.

A few hours later and we'd already given hugs to Rachel at the door, high-fived the man with a Mohawk, and chatted with my friend Peter who runs the kombucha stand. We were in the middle of the dance floor, sweaty arms around each other, laughing as we mimicked each other's dance moves. At one point, I did a fake rebirth of Laura where she slid dramatically between my legs as other people did jazz hands all around her. It was bonkers, and ended in a group hug.

After I broke away from the sea of arms, Duncan put both hands on my shoulders. "Jill!" he yelled. "I am so proud of you!"

For a moment, I was confused. Was the friend rebirth that good?

But then I realized what he meant—how much I've changed since I was paralyzed underneath that disco ball in the East Village.

I found The Get Down and actively chose to make it a community that would facilitate my transformation. Now,

I show up at the events, promote them, and go to dinner parties with the team. I'm even friends with Tasha, the DJ who I could barely make eye contact with because she so fully represented the embodied confidence I longed to have.

Eventually we would facilitate a Joy List event together—which included dance.

A good event can create a temporary sense of belonging. Yet a great event creates the conditions for someone to step into leadership and feel a sense of community that was created by deeply owning their experience in the space. I stepped up to that challenge and was rewarded with a true feeling of contribution and belonging.

I'll fully admit, I'm still not a great dancer. But I am an enthusiastic one.

CREATING THE WORLD WE WANT TO SEE

Events can be church.

How many times have you been at a gathering and wished you were somewhere else? That thought crosses my mind almost any time I'm at a networking event, conference, or panel. There's this feeling that the organizer phoned it in. Somebody gave them a template, and they copied it.

Whenever I sense this, it genuinely hurts me. Bringing people together, whether it's for a 100th birthday or a company happy hour, is a sacred opportunity. Whether you know it or not, the people in that room want to feel like someone cares about them enough to create a special environment. Yet all too often, this chance to help people feel valued and connected is wasted.

Why? Because we think too small.

Gathering together is an opportunity to create an alternate universe. And when someone enters that space, you will forever shift their perspective on what is possible.

As Priya Parker argues in *The Art of Gathering*, we should create a temporary alternative world in our spaces. "A gathering's blandness is a symptom of a disease," she says. "And what is the disease? That the gathering makes no effort to do what the best gatherings do: transport us to a temporary alternative world."

"How We Gather," a 2015 report by three Harvard Divinity School alumni, dives into how Millennials are finding and building community.[25] The research, conducted by Angie Thurston, Casper ter Kuile and Sue Phillips, shines a light on how desperate young people are to find spaces where they feel like a part of something that's bigger than themselves.

Now, in 2019, "How We Gather" has transformed into a "ground-breaking study of organizations that are effectively unbundling and remixing the functions historically performed by traditional religious institutions."

One of their recent reports, "Something More," hit an emotional chord with me that I couldn't quite put a finger on.[26] Only after some reflection did I realize that their team had summarized in a sentence what I'd been experiencing in New York City for a couple of years. As they explain, "The constructed categories of what is 'religious' and what is 'secular' are no longer the most helpful ways to understand how we are gathering and making meaning of our lives."

That rang true for me. Organized religion is not the way I—or many Americans—find guidance, purpose, or consistent connection. Yet at the same time, we still need healthy congregation. We still need a space that, as the "How We Gather" authors put it, has "something more."

With that in mind, here's the crucial question: what ingredients are necessary to make those gatherings possible?

THE SIX RULES TO TRANSFORMATION

As the founder of The Joy List, I've curated hundreds of events that facilitate connection. I'm constantly in conversations about what allows a space to transform its guests—and attempt to apply those learnings to my own gatherings.

After looking through the events I've highlighted the most frequently in my newsletter, I've found six key themes that take an event from mundane to a congregation that has the potential to change people's lives:

1) **Behavior modeling:** At all of my favorite events, the organizer models the type of behavior they want to see in their participants. If they want their guests to share vulnerably in a circle, they stand in front of the room and offer a story of a time they struggled. If they want their guests to be playful, they're the first to start busting out the crazy dance moves.

In doing so, the event leader shows the room that this environment is a brave space. While it's impossible to promise that nothing bad will happen and that no one's feelings will be hurt, it is possible to show trust in the room. By sharing a vulnerable story, the leader is essentially saying, "I trust you to hold this. While you might not give me the exact response I need, I trust that your intention was different than your impact."

Of course, the leader isn't always in the right headspace to create the intended environment. Maybe they feel too sick to dance or are grieving the loss of a relative and don't feel comfortable sharing with their dinner party. In this case, it's up to their team members and volunteers to step up. For example, at The Get Down, Tasha Blank doesn't even dance. After all, she's the DJ! Instead, she has a team of people she knows will be there every time. We set the stage for people to feel comfortable getting weird. So if you're a gatherer, have no fear. The pressure to create the space should not just be on your shoulders.

2) Clear "hurdle" rules: Any event that's worth going to has at least one rule that will make some people uncomfortable. This could be no drinking, no phones, or everyone has to wear a onesie. This serves a dual purpose—it gets people out of their comfort zone while also giving attendees the knowledge that they have at least one thing in common with everyone there. The types of people who didn't want to be in a sober space on a Friday night didn't show up!

3) Unity through the obvious: A great facilitator provides a sense of unity by calling out what should be completely apparent but often isn't considered. For example, "You all gave your Saturday—half of your weekend—to be at this conference. That's how much everyone in this room cares about ethical technology."

4) Greeting with intention: The most memorable events are thoughtfully designed from the start. Once attendees enter, they should be greeted with kindness and a reminder of the rules. I love when there is something tangible and intangible as part of this greeting. For example, it's lovely to be met with a piece of chocolate or a cup of tea at the door. It's also important to feel the kindness of the person doing the greeting, and their genuine gladness that you're there.

If many people at your event don't know each other, it's also wonderful for a volunteer to introduce every guest to someone new. Bonus points if they provide an icebreaker that can be used for future conversations. For example, "What's something that brought you joy today?" "What was the last thing you ate for the first time?" or "What's something that you need help with right now?"

5) Closing with a call to the future: It's easy for an event organizer to feel burned out by the final minutes of a gathering. As a result, it's tempting to thank the venue and sponsors as quickly as possible and then get the hell out of there. Yet, as Priya Parker notes in *The Art of Gathering*, people's strongest memories of an event are the beginning and the end.

Use this precious time to tell your guests how you hope this gathering will change the way they interact with the world. That could range from something simple like, "I hope you leave here with a business connection you're excited to follow up with" to something a little more action-oriented like, "After today I hope you decide to bring more play into your day."

Your guests just experienced something you designed for them. Let them know how you hope it impacts their life.

6) Levels of leadership: If someone loves your event, let them help! Small events should have volunteer opportunities for promotion, brand partnerships, setup, greeting, and breakdown. Large events should scale beyond that and create committees. A great resource for learning about this organizational structure is *The Art of Community* by Charles Vogl.

Looking for more help? Check out www.joylist.nyc/resources for our crowd-sourced collection of community-building tools.

WE TRUST WHAT TRANSFORMS

Back in 2015, Matt Salandra was not in a good place. The woman he wanted to marry had just broken up with him, he was feeling uninspired at his job, and he was not comfortable in his body. "I had no idea what to do," Matt told me. "I was showing up to work late. I wasn't productive. I was self-conscious about my appearance."

Around that time, Matt was invited to a seminar hosted by Tony Robbins, a world-renowned self-help guru who's sold out arenas and is the founder of several companies that earn approximately $5 billion in annual sales.[27] The invitation came from a colleague Matt admired—the kind of man who was financially successful and ran multiple businesses. Matt wanted to be like him. So, even though he knew almost nothing about the self-help guru—except that he once made an appearance in the movie *Shallow Hal*—Matt said yes. He was ready to grab onto anything that could help him out of his funk. A weekend called "Unleash the Power Within" seemed like a good bet.

To use some personal development terminology, Matt really "showed up" on the first morning of the event. He arrived at 7:30 a.m. and was one of the first people to check in. He then stood in the snow, waiting with over five thousand people, for two more hours. Finally, the crowd slowly started to file into the stadium.

At that point, Matt still had over an hour to wait. And then, at last, the lights started to dim. A group walked onto the stage, but it wasn't Tony. It was his dancers. "My friend and I looked at each other, like 'What are they doing?'" Matt recalled. And then, to his horror, they asked everyone to get out of their seat and start dancing.

Matt remained firmly planted in his chair—but the people around him were *into it.* One woman in front of him was dancing so freely, and with so much energy, that Matt was convinced—just like me at The Get Down—that she was on drugs. "I'd never seen anything like it," Matt laughed. "I was wondering what the hell I'd gotten myself into."

Ten minutes go by. Matt is still cemented in his chair, watching everyone around him boogie their faces off. Eventually, he stands up, sways awkwardly, and starts to clap. To his relief, the lights finally go down, the dramatic music swells, and the God of self-help, Tony Robbins, runs onstage. The arena explodes with cheers and screams.

Once everyone calms down, Tony tells everyone in the audience to give ten strangers a hug. Matt is uncomfortable, but he does it.

With that, the event has officially begun.

"I had my big breakthrough on the last day," Matt told me. Tony was showing a video about factory farming and talking about the importance of taking care of your health. In that moment, Matt's chair made a strange noise...and then snapped in half. Matt hit the floor, chair pieces flying around him. Volunteers scattered, trying to find him a stronger, reinforced seat.

"I wasn't even thinking about my health at the start of the weekend," Matt told me. "I wanted to learn skills to help me run my own business." He didn't consciously think that changing his health would improve his happiness. Yet without even trying, Matt lost five pounds during the three-day program. After that, he took Tony's ten-day nutrition challenge and dropped fifteen more.

Cut to three years later, and Matt has lost over one hundred pounds, volunteers for Tony Robbins, and is frequently a paid consultant for his events.

He is all Tony, all the time.

"I go to his events, back to back to back," Matt told me. "They remind me that I'm in charge of my life. Going to these events is like going to the gym, but for success."

Why are these people so committed to spreading Tony's message? Because they become obsessed with the thing that facilitates their transformation.

When I asked Matt why he decided to start working with Tony's team, his answer surprised me: "To end human suffering."

Turns out, every single one of the four hundred to six hundred people who volunteer during a Tony Robbins event are unified under that goal. As Matt explained, "We want to serve his mission to help as many people in their transformation as possible."

Tony himself explains why so many people are happy to help him in his quest to help others. During the last few minutes of his TED talk, Robbins drops this line of wisdom: "People get excited to contribute when they get the chance to experience it, not talk about it." Rather than making empty promises, volunteers for his events have an actionable way to create change both for other people and within themselves.

While attending a Tony event is very oriented toward individual change, volunteering is all about serving a larger purpose. "The community's definitely a family," Matt said. "We support each other."

During our conversation, he told me about some fellow crew members who had emotional breakthroughs and talked about things with him that they didn't even tell their own family members. "I've developed some of my closest friends through that," Matt said. "We know it's a safe space. I'd say that being part of the crew is more powerful than just attending the event itself."

FINDING YOUR ALTERNATE UNIVERSE

At this point, you're probably excited to find your alternate universe. Yet if you don't live in New York City, you can't go to The Get Down. And if you're not into self-help or have a small events budget, you won't be going to Tony Robbins anytime soon. So what can you do?

Your life will get better the moment you prioritize spaces that allow for a different version of reality. Since you might have no idea where to begin, I've created a simple, three-step process to get you started:

1) Go into discovery mode: There are plenty of great events out there. You simply need to know where to look. I recommend curation platforms like Kinvite and Deepen, Facebook and Eventbrite's discovery features, and event-sourcing newsletters like TimeOut and—shameless plug—The Joy List.

2) Get out the door: While this is easy to say, it's also difficult to do. Embarking on a new adventure is scary—especially if you go by yourself. Yet it's worth the risk. I promise.

Worst-case scenario, you have a great story to tell. Best-case scenario, you find a new group of people who will become your chosen family.

If you already feel lonely, leaving the house is the most difficult step. You're probably having thoughts like, "No one will like me there anyways" or "They don't really want me to go." Yet this is perfectly normal. In fact, it's scientifically proven that our brain's perception of reality is different when we're lonely. As John T. Cacioppo and William Patrick say in their book, *Loneliness*, protracted loneliness makes it difficult for us to evaluate other people's intentions. This can lead to social awkwardness as well as defensiveness. Why? Lonely people often feel attacked in situations that are actually neutral. As the authors say, "These negative expectations then have a way of becoming self-fulfilling prophecies."[28]

The solution is to—no matter what your mind is telling you—trust that people have your best interest at heart. They are genuinely glad you are joining them. While this might be difficult, or even impossible to believe at first, remember that your brain is playing tricks on you. It wants you to believe that no one wants to spend time with you in order to keep you trapped in a cycle of loneliness. Only you have the power to break out of it, even if your mind is saying that leaving the comfort of home will only result in disaster. I've been there and can tell you from the other side that there are some pretty amazing people out here. And we're excited to meet you.

3) **Flex the muscle:** Doing new things takes practice. There will be times when you go to something that's not your scene. Do not—I repeat, *do not*—let this dissuade you from further adventures in the future. It took me a *year* of consistently attending events by myself in New York to find spaces and relationships where I truly feel like I belong. Yet now I have a level of depth in my relationships, and a connection to my community, that is unfortunately rare.

Be one of those people who flexes your "new things" muscle. As a wise doctor named Seuss once said: "If you never did, you should. These things are fun and fun is good." While it's scary to get out of your comfort zone, I can promise you will be rewarded. My life in New York City now is the direct result of putting myself in new situations over and over again.

CREATE THE SPACE YOU WANT TO SEE

"Trump is going forward with the Muslim ban."

Those words froze a room of four hundred college leaders in their tracks.

The group was at the Interfaith Core Leadership Institute training, an amazing yearly conference that brings young people from all faiths together to have challenging conversations about religion and politics. These students learn how to facilitate conversations on their college campuses between groups that disagree. They are trained for respectful interfaith cooperation. In other words, they have the skills that all of us should learn in school... but don't.

The annual conference also happened to be where the students learned that Donald Trump was— as a news release from his campaign said— "calling for a total and complete shutdown of Muslims entering the United States until our country's representatives can figure out what is going on."

Katie Gordon, one of the facilitators, watched as atheist, Christian, Muslim, and Jewish students started to panic. The room buzzed with fearful questions: "Are the airports safe?" "How can we travel?" "What does this mean for my family?"

Katie remembers this moment as one of great difficulty, yet also of powerful solidarity. "In that instant, it was natural for them to come together," she told me. "For many of the Christian students, it was their first time seeing the impact of this sort of Muslim persecution up close."

Calls started coming in from parents, especially those with hijab-wearing daughters. They wanted to know if their children were safe. Many requested that they come home immediately. Others told their kids to stay in town for as long as necessary. They didn't want them to risk stepping foot into an airport and being deported.

On the last day of the conference, Katie went to the airport with three young women, one of whom was Muslim and wearing a hijab. Together, the group walked past hundreds of people chanting. Katie and her students stuck close together. They never left each other as they walked towards the gate.

"Her parents were so afraid for her to be traveling that day," Katie told me. "And her travel companions fully supported her and showed up for her. I'll never forget that moment."

Katie told me that the highest calling of interfaith leadership is to build community across religious and secular traditions. Their goal is to create a common shared leadership narrative for everyone to unite under, regardless of background.

That moment in the airport is a representation of that mission in action. They created the space they wanted to see, and those values traveled outside the conference center walls.

A great measure of the impact a space has is how people react to and talk about it. For example, Katie still gets passionate when she discusses that interfaith summit. Tasha gets emotional when she talks about the power of dance. I start to cry when I think about Camp Grounded and how Levi died so young.

For a while it was hard for me to understand why I'm so emotionally attached to an experience that involved someone I had never met. Yet now, I realize it's because I deeply value how he could allow people to drop their walls and connect. His creation helped me learn that events can create an alternate universe, shift our perspective, and allow people to choose what learnings they bring into the outside world.

KEY TAKEAWAYS

- People are loyal to the event that facilitates their transformation.
- A good event can create a temporary sense of belonging. Yet a great event creates the conditions for someone to step into leadership and feel a sense of community that was created by deeply owning their experience in the space.
- Events can create an alternate universe, shift our perspective, and allow people to choose what learnings they will bring into the outside world.

- To start finding your new alternate realities, you need to go into discovery mode, get out the door, and keep flexing your "trying new things" muscle.

QUESTIONS TO CONSIDER

- How can we create transformative spaces that continue to foster the growth of old members while also being welcoming enough for new people to join?
- How can the organizers of transformative spaces get paid well without relying on the potentially unhealthy power dynamic of asking current members to refer new people?
- What type of promotion is most appropriate for gatherings that rely on attendees feeling safe? How can we portray the gathering's power without breaking the trust of attendees?

4

SHARING WITH STRANGERS

"A city like London is sociable in a sense that there are people gathering in bars and restaurants, concerts and lectures. Yet you can partake of all these experiences and never say hello to anyone new. And one of the things that all religions do is take groups of strangers into a space and say it is okay to talk to each other."

—ALAIN DE BOTTON

"I think my partner and I are going to call off our engagement."

A room of people sitting on meditation cushions received these words with respectful silence.

The man speaking explained that he and his partner had been in couples counseling for a few months. That week was the first time they admitted that their relationship simply wasn't going to work.

My heart hurt for this stranger.

When he was finished talking, there was a stillness as the room took a few silent breaths together. No one offered him advice.

Finally, someone said "Thank you," and another person began to share what was going on in their life. With that, the room's full attention turned to them.

By the end of the evening, I had the honor of hearing some deeply personal stories from complete strangers. People dove into struggles with self-confidence, battles with addiction, and impostor syndrome at work. It struck me that I never would have known about our similarities if I was just passing them on the sidewalk outside—yet I shared a lot of their problems.

I started attending this event, known as Balanced NYC, on a weekly basis in 2016. It was originally run in the Soho apartment of Casey Rosengren, the founder of Hacker Paradise, and Leo Widrich, the cofounder of Buffer. Their home was cozy and—rare for New York—the entire floor of a building. They had space for dozens of people to get together and, bless them, they used it.

Every gathering began with a group meditation, followed by a short talk and a longer group conversation. I feel lucky that Balanced was one of my first meditation experiences. It was a welcoming and accessible space to learn about cultivating mindfulness. The experience also introduced me to some of my closest friends in the city—including Dennis, my now-roommate. (He also happens to be the man who shared about his impending separation.)

Every time I emerged from their events, I didn't just feel connected to the people in the space. I also felt a sense of caring for everyone passing by me on the street. In fact, I even started to notice that more people smiled at me after a Balanced meditation. Of course, passersby probably noticed how open I seemed and shot me a smile because it felt welcomed. Yet at the same time, I genuinely believe I had friendlier interactions with everyone around me because I was conscious of how interconnected we all are.

This sense of openness was largely due to how well-organized Balanced was. Casey and Leo created a structure, followed it, and allowed other community members to take leadership. In fact, every week was facilitated by a different person. The theme could be anything from "play" to "grief," as long as it connected to the person's own life. As a result, Balanced didn't just feel like a space where we went and received information. It was a healthy congregation.

For those of you who might want to replicate the event, here's the breakdown of the structure.

The elevator doors open, and you're greeted by a member of the community. They invite you to take off your shoes and then offer a pair of slippers and a cup of tea. People mill about, add Post-its to a gratitude wall, and chat until the gong is rung. At this point, everyone heads into the living room and chooses a meditation cushion to sit on.

To ground the group after a hectic day of New York City life, either Casey or Leo leads a twenty-minute meditation. This could be anything from a loving-kindness practice to a reflection on death. Afterward, the guest speaker for the week reads from their chosen text and shares a personal story that connects to the theme.

After that, we get into groups of three and reflect on how the topic relates to our own lives. Each person gets two uninterrupted minutes to speak. Everyone else just listens.

While this sounds simple, it's rare to be in conversation for that long without interrupting. The next time you're talking with someone, notice how long it takes until you feel the urge to jump in and offer your opinion or advice. Chances are, it's not even sixty seconds. With this discussion framework, the speaker gets to be deeply heard while their group members experience what it feels like to deeply listen.

Once everyone has spoken in their small circles, the room returns to a full group conversation. Participants can share what stood out to them in their conversation. This moment gives them the opportunity to be witnessed and accepted by the entire room, no matter what they bring. It's a powerful experience that brings meditators back week after week.

As Dennis told me years later at our own apartment, "It felt like walking into my home. I knew people there. It was warm."

Yet as happens with all communities, things had to change eventually. This happened at Balanced a year after I joined. We were all sitting together, waiting for Casey to share the theme for the evening. I noticed that he looked overwhelmed as he took a deep breath. "Everyone," he told the group. "I'll be moving to Japan in a few weeks. Leo will be moving to Austria to live in a monastery. That means this is one of the last few Balanced that we'll host."

The room was shocked. I looked at Dennis and mouthed a dramatic, "*Noooooooo!*" from across the room. He nodded in agreement. Later that night, as we had our traditional post-meditation salad, we hatched a plan.

Cut to a few weeks later. It's the last session of Balanced, and Casey and Leo's living room is packed with fifty people. "This event has meant so much to me," Casey said. "Leo and I created it because we wanted a sense of community. We didn't want to be lonely anymore. And you all made that possible. By showing up every week, you made this feel like the first place where I was really at home."

There was not a dry eye in sight.

With that, Casey looked at me and Dennis and grinned, adding, "But thankfully, things don't have to end here."

Someone gasped. From one corner another person yelled, "What?"

I smiled and looked at the room, heart racing. "When Dennis and I heard that Balanced was ending, we were devastated," I said. "Coming here feels like walking into a warm hug. And we couldn't let that end. So Dennis and I are moving into our own apartment together, and we're bringing Balanced with us."

We literally did. The couches, lamps, and tables from that meditation studio all became part of our new home. With that setup in place, we started hosting Balanced in our apartment. From week one, it was an amazing experience. People we had never even met would come and share their souls with us. Every time, no fail, I would be reminded of how I am not alone in my problems. I would remember how everyone is connected.

SCREW "STRANGER DANGER"

As Brené Brown says in her book, *Daring Greatly,* fear stops us from connecting with each other. "Fear of vulnerability. Fear of getting hurt. Fear of the pain of disconnection. Fear of criticism and failure. Fear of conflict. Fear of not measuring up. Fear."[29]

Bravery allows us to move past that bullshit and create a state of empowered belonging.

Brené has found in her research that the people who have the strongest sense of belonging don't reach out to others occasionally. Instead, they have formed a habit of getting vulnerable and asking for connection consistently.

As she argues, "True belonging is not passive... It's a practice that requires us to be vulnerable, get uncomfortable, and learn how to be present with people without sacrificing who we are. We want true belonging, but it takes tremendous courage to knowingly walk into hard moments."

I've experienced this intimately. In my first year in New York, I went to over one hundred events alone. I was on a quest to find my people. Sure, I moved through a lot of uncomfortable moments in those gatherings—and it was worth it. Since I put time and energy into finding the people who light me up, I now have the strongest relationships of my life.

Yet it wasn't always that way. The first time I walked into Medi Club, a monthly meditation and social event in NYC, I felt like I had stumbled into a Free People ad. While I thought I was in for a chill hangout like Balanced, I had no idea that this was a total cool kid scene. Everyone was gorgeous, thin, and a walking combination of linen, floppy hats, and palo santo smoke. With my thrift store clothes and curvy body, I was intimidated to say the least. That intimidation made me judgmental.

"They all look so cool," I thought. "Why would they want to talk to me?"

Thankfully, Medi Club is the type of event I promote in The Joy List. Every gathering, they include multiple facilitated moments of connection. We dance together, say hi to our neighbors, and have small group conversations. That evening, the prompt was, "What's an old story you have about yourself that you want to leave in the past?" Fittingly, I confessed to my triad that I wanted to abandon the idea that I'm not meant to be in "cool" spaces, no matter how well-intentioned they are. To my total shock, the man to my left—AKA one of the most gorgeous people I'd ever seen—said that he felt the exact same way.

This moment reinforced the lesson I keep relearning again and again. No matter what my problem is, I'm not alone.

Conversations with strangers allow us to share things about ourselves that we wouldn't discuss with our friends or family. Since the other person doesn't have any pre-existing stories about us, we can speak freely. They are not "too close."

These discussions also remind us of our shared humanity. Whenever I'm preoccupied with my own problems, a good chat with a group reminds me that I'm not alone in my struggles—and that other people are moving through more. This is especially important for the many Americans who are lonely and have not yet established close friendships that allow them to share vulnerably. In fact, facilitated conversations are a great place to create new relationships.

There's a reason why sharing with strangers is so powerful. They're actually likely to understand us more than people we know. As Nicholas Epley, a professor of behavioral science at the University of Chicago Booth School of Business, said in an article for Consumer Affairs, "Our problem in communicating with friends and spouses is that we have an illusion of insight. Getting close to someone appears to create the illusion of understanding more than actual understanding."[30]

In other words, people are thinking more about themselves when they talk to a friend. They don't consider the option that their friend has the same information they have. "The understanding, 'What I know is different from what you know' is essential for effective communication to occur," Kenneth Savitsky, a professor of psychology at Williams College, added. "It is necessary for giving directions, for teaching a class or just for having an ordinary conversation. But that insight can be elusive when the 'you' in question is a close friend or spouse."

After that night at Medi Club, I volunteered to set up chairs at every event for a year. While the good-looking people honestly did have a little bit to do with it, I also wanted to support a container for strangers to be vulnerable with each other. If the founders, Jesse Israel and Lauren Bille, hadn't given my group permission to drop our walls and have an honest conversation, I would have continued my assumption that everyone was part of this clique but me. In reality, many people felt the same way I did.

The following year, I was helping set up for The Big Quiet, a mass meditation that's run by the Medi Club team. This gathering, held at the top of One World Trade, was especially moving. Religious leaders from multiple faiths came together and led us in song and meditation. We shared with strangers. We remembered that, even when we are told we have differences that should divide us, we always share more things that bring us together. Looking out at the skyline of New York City that night, surrounded by a thousand fellow meditators, I had a deep longing for more spaces where people can come together across divisions. That's the world I want to co-create.

CREATE CONVERSATION AGREEMENTS

Any event that includes a partnered share or group conversation should have a set of standards for how people behave. While this might seem like overkill, they're the perfect touchpoint when someone is being disruptive, intentionally or not.

Make use of the guidelines below in order to create the space you wish to see in the world:

1) Speak from the I: When I share vulnerably, I desperately want to distance myself from the personal nature of what I'm saying. That's when I'll speak in the "you." Personally, it's easier to say, "You know when you go on a date with someone, and you can tell that they're not attracted to you? That can be really hard." This distancing from my own personal experience is a defense mechanism—and a super common one. I'm working on unlearning the behavior.

In order to take ownership for my experience, I need to learn to rephrase my story to be in the "I." To use the previous example, I would change my share to be: "I went on a date with someone and I could tell that he wasn't attracted to me. It was really hard." This feels more raw, which is exactly what should be happening in a space that's created for brave conversations.

Pro tip: If you have some attendees who are constantly speaking in the "you," make up a gesture to remind them to rephrase their sentence. I personally like pointing to my eyeball. I've seen other facilitators simply say "I" out loud until the person gets the message. It sounds obnoxious, but it's an important way for the attendee to really feel what they're experiencing. Once I asked a woman in my circle to start speaking in the "I." The moment she did, she started tearing up, which helped her come to terms with how she was really feeling, rather than distancing herself from the experience.

2) Be mindful of time: If you're lucky, everyone at your gathering will be excited to speak. The only problem with this situation is that someone can hog the mic and completely take over the conversation. To (hopefully) curtail this, remind everyone at the start of your event to be mindful of time. A line I like to use is, "Please share what's on your heart, and remember that we want everyone to have the opportunity to speak."

This rule requires the most masterful facilitating. If someone is really going on a tangent, interrupt and do one of two things:

- Ask them to summarize their story in three sentences or less.
- Tell them that it sounds like their experience is complicated, and you'd love to hear the full story after the event. Unfortunately, you have to be mindful of time and give other people in the room the opportunity to speak.

While you might feel like the bad cop, know the other people in the room are grateful. Even if you temporarily offend someone, you are honoring the intention you set for the space and ensuring everyone else feels like their time and presence is valued.

3) No advice: Americans love giving advice. It's part of our culture. Yet while people have great intentions—they want to be helpful!—offering suggestions on how to change is typically the *last* thing people want to hear when they're sharing from their heart. There's a reason the cliché therapist line is, "How does that make you feel?" versus, "Here's what I think you should do."

As we established before, events are the perfect opportunity to create an alternate universe. Let yours be one where people can simply feel heard and witnessed, rather than like they need to be fixed.

To establish this boundary, I recommend saying: "Today, we won't be giving advice unless someone has specifically asked for it. You'll know you're giving advice if you tell someone how to fix their situation rather than sitting with them and getting curious about how they feel." While this might sound easy, you'll be surprised by how many times you'll want to jump into a discussion to offer a "solution."

Giving advice makes us feel important. Listening helps the other person feel important.

4) What's shared here, stays here: People will never share vulnerably if they think their story is going to be gossiped about later. For that reason, establish the rule that whatever is said in the room, stays there.

To take that boundary a step further, add that people might not want to talk about what they shared in the circle at a later time.

For example, if someone shares about the grief they're feeling over their father passing, you should ask if you can discuss the topic with them once the circle has closed. They might feel complete after sharing it once and don't want to continue the conversation any further. By asking, you ensure that someone isn't getting into a discussion they never wanted to have in the first place.

5) Listen deeply: How often have you been in a conversation where it felt like no one was actually listening to each other?

Having spent a lot of time with comedians, I can personally say it's exhausting.

To create a space where people feel respected, encourage deep listening. This means being present while someone shares... without interrupting them. That's right—the other person speaks while you offer absolutely no commentary at all.

Be warned: this will feel weird. Yet I encourage you, and your attendees, to feel into that awkwardness. When do you feel discomfort? Why? Use it as a teaching opportunity.

An easy way to create this space is to set a timer for each person. I typically allow each person two minutes and then give the small group four or five minutes to talk amongst themselves.

This rule once made such an impact on a woman and her partner that they came up and told me they'd never listened so closely to each other in the years of their relationship. That comment speaks volumes about how conditioned we are to think about whatever we're going to say next rather than being curious about the experience of the other person.

6) No cross-talk: This rule is better for large groups, yet is similar to "listen deeply." It simply means that one person should speak at a time, with no one talking over them or starting a side conversation.

7) Speak from the heart, not from the head: My friend Duncan created this rule for himself at his dinner series. As he says at the start of the meal, "To avoid conversations about my own emotions, I get philosophical and heady. So tonight, we will avoid talking about what Proust theory we think applies to the discussion. Instead, we'll focus on our personal experiences and how we feel."

This brings the conversation to a much more personal level and allows the guests to learn more about each other's inner worlds—rather than academic musings that fail to foster connection.

7:47 CLUB

In July 2015, Chris Schembra returned to the US after producing a Broadway play in Italy.

From that description alone, you'd assume he was on top of the world. He had a successful career, was traveling the world, and was getting paid to do what he loved. Yet transitioning from his tight-knit theater community to the isolation of his one-bedroom apartment in Soho made him feel extremely lonely.

"I was insecure, disconnected, and unfulfilled," Chris told me. "My greatest insecurity growing up was that I knew so many different diverse groups of people, but I was always the last one called to the party. People said, 'Why call Chris? He's probably already taken care of by another group." As an adult, Chris felt the same lack of tribe.

Then, pasta sauce changed everything.

Chris loves to cook. So, one weekend, he decided to experiment with making a pasta sauce. Since it was pretty good, he invited fifteen friends over to try it.

Once they arrived, Chris delegated tasks for his friends to do. Some helped set the table, others made the peanut butter sauce for the ice cream. Then, over the course of the next few hours, they talked. By the end of the night, a few people had cried. That's when Chris knew he was onto something and decided to do the same exact thing the following week.

Three hundred and sixty-five days later, Chris had hosted the 7:47 Club—named after the exact time the first dinner started—fifty-two times. He hadn't skipped hosting the meal once for an entire year. Over eight hundred people have been fed in his home.

Then, at around 2:00 a.m. on a Monday in February of 2016, Chris shot up in bed. "I started bawling my eyes out," he told me. "I realized for the first time in my life that I was feeling a little bit of joy. I was starting to lose my insecurities."

When he was younger, Chris hated being the last one invited to the party. Yet now he'd flipped that story on its head and was the person creating the safe spaces for others.

"In that moment in bed, I started to realize the joy in that experience," Chris said. "I started realizing I was creating transformative moments."

Now businesses pay Chris to host these dinners for their business leads and to teach them how to throw the dinners on their own.

In other words, he is one of the rare people on this planet who is making good money *and* creating a loving space for connection. Chris can sit down with a venture capitalist, drop a bunch of statistics about how authentic conversations can convert to business, and sell a pack of twelve dinners within the hour. In other words, he has made vulnerability into a business—and I'm jealous I didn't think of it first.

"When you can create an emotional connection with your prospect, they're 50 percent more likely to buy," Chris told me. "By understanding what problems you can solve in that person's personal life, you can add value for the client. These dinners were really all about that personal connection. We don't have our clients giving a pitch. They're just there to increase touch points and listen to their clients' personal aspirations. It's a building of energy and emotional connection."

The evening starts at 6:30 p.m. with a cocktail hour. Sixteen strangers in suits mingle, make small talk, and clink glasses. They don't know what's about to hit them.

At 7:47, Chris pairs people up and assigns eleven different tasks: set the table, make the sauce for the ice cream, portion out the pasta. "We're empowering the attendees to work together to create the meal," Chris said. "That creates connection."

By the time people sit down for dinner, everyone is warmed up and ready to dive into a deeper conversation. So, after explaining the timeline for the night, Chris drops the night's question on his guests:

"If you could give credit or thanks to one person in your life that you don't give enough credit or thanks to, who would it be?"

At one dinner, a client said they would give more thanks to their younger brother. "I grew up in a household where we didn't show love or affection, especially verbally," he said. "My younger brother has no idea how much he means to me."

A few weeks later, Chris ran into that guest on the street. It turns out, 7:47 Club inspired him to get in his car, drive upstate, and visit his brother for the first time in his life.

At a different meal, two men—who arrived separately—both came out as gay for the first time in their lives.

Powerful stuff for a business dinner, right?

Chris told me that one of his mentors inspired how he markets the dinner. He purposefully masks the offering in something that's comfortably sellable to his customer: client engagement, team building, leadership development. He gets them in the door with that—and then they leave with so much more.

"Our dinners help people find the comfort of family," Chris said. "Because whether people in the corporate sector realize it or not, they are craving empathy, vulnerability, and maternal energy. Our dinners help them feel that."

My last question to Chris was this: "Do you see a similarity between the reasons why people would come to 7:47 Club and why people attend church?"

His answer was so well-said that I want to provide it in its entirety:

"When you think about prayer, prayer doesn't come from the preacher. The preacher just inspires and facilitates the discussion around wisdom passed down from elders.

When I create a shared group experience like 7:47 Club, I'm not taking the spotlight. I'm the facilitator. I'm leading from behind and empowering the attendees to share their voice. That creates wisdom.

We live in an age where the transfer of wisdom is less prevalent. We used to have these matriarchal societies where the people would sit around the elders and listen to the tales of history. History is our greatest teacher and we would be fools to turn our backs on it. That's why we need leaders to step up and create those experiences for the transfer of wisdom and stories and history. That in itself is modern day prayer."

Chris found his life's mission through serving people. "Our community has been built because of a shared experience," he said. "No matter when people show up at a 7:47 Club, you're going to get a curated event that is designed to create the same group dynamic."

Throughout the course of its existence, many 7:47 Club conversations have inspired people to change their lives. Before one dinner, Chris texted a woman who'd expressed interest in attending. She received the message when she was driving to JFK for a vacation—and she turned around. This woman willingly cancelled her vacation in order to go to a dinner party.

"She told me that she needed this energy," Chris said. After that 7:47 Club, she quit her finance job, went back to business school, and started volunteering for a lot of nonprofit boards. She made the choice to bring more joy into her life.

Overwhelmingly, the response to Chris's "Who would you thank?" question is, "My mom." This answer has helped Chris tap into the reason why his dinners are such a catalyst for people to connect and create change in their lives.

"If 7:47 Club was a gender, it would be a woman," Chris told me. "Because what I realized through hosting these dinners is that people are craving maternal energy and empathy."

BEING BRAVE IN YOUR SPACE

The next time you attend an event, look around. Then ask yourself: "How many people in this space are like me? And in what ways?"

Before I became passionate about community building, I honestly never thought about the demographic makeup of the rooms I entered. Yet, once I started to see through that lens, I began to notice how little diversity existed in the spaces I inhabited. My circle was largely white, progressive people between the ages of twenty-two and thirty-five who were "spiritual but not religious," worked for themselves, and listened to some combination of the Tim Ferriss, On Being, and SuperSoul Sunday podcasts. We labeled ourselves "personal development nerds," went on meditation retreats, and attended men's or women's circles on a regular basis.

While I adore my friends, the homogeneity of my group disturbed me. I realized if I didn't make the conscious choice to change who I surrounded myself with, I could socialize with the same types of people *forever.*

Why is that bad? Well, being surrounded by sameness means that my beliefs will never be strongly challenged because the people around me share the same worldview. As a result, I won't have to defend my opinions, and I'll miss an opportunity to both work through how I truly feel and see both sides of an argument from a more nuanced perspective. Sameness means I will rarely have to confront my privilege, both economically and racially, because I seldom brush up against the uncomfortable edges of someone's experience being less advantageous than mine. For example, it's easy to say, "Let's go to Sweetgreen for lunch!" and eat some salad with friends, without thinking about the cost of the meal. I also won't have a moment of questioning when most of the people in line are white, and most of the servers are black.

Sameness means I can surround myself with young entrepreneurs who are passionate about "making it" in a capitalist system without wondering why we feel like checking everything off our to-do list will mean we're worthy of love. Sameness means I can sit with a circle of young women and talk about our relationship problems yet never get the insight of someone who has lived for twice as long as we have and has seen some shit that she's willing to share.

Once I had my "aha" moment, I knew that I had two choices. I could either stay in my circle, or actively diversify the people I surround myself with. That's why I made a New Year's resolution to broaden my friend group. And to be honest, it's been the most difficult goal to achieve, both because it's uncomfortable to talk about and easy to avoid.

This topic begs the question: does staying within sameness actually fuel a sense of disconnection?

In *Braving the Wilderness*, Brené Brown draws a connection between the rising political polarization in the United States and the amount of loneliness.[31] First, she cites data from researcher, Robert Bishop:

"In 1976 less than 25 percent of Americans lived in places where the presidential election was a landslide. In other words, we lived next door to, and attended school and worshiped with, people who held different beliefs than ours. We were ideologically diverse. In contrast, in 2016, 80 percent of US

counties gave either Donald Trump or Hillary Clinton a landslide victory. Most of us no longer even live near people who are all that different from us in terms of political and social beliefs."

Data has proven that staying within sameness does not actually create a sense of belonging. Rather, it fuels feelings of isolation. This is supported by researcher, Bill Bishop, in his 2009 book, *The Big Sort:*

"As people seek out the social settings they prefer—as they choose the group that makes them feel the most comfortable—the nation grows more politically segregated—and the benefit that ought to come with having a variety of opinions is lost to the righteousness that is the special entitlement of homogeneous groups."[32]

To quote a popular phrase from the media, we live in a bubble that only allows for dialogue with people we're comfortable with, and who share similar life experiences. Anything outside of that is easily shut out.

Yet even if you realize you want to expand your friend network, it's hard to know where to start.

I suggest beginning where every great quest begins—with a public ask on social media.

But seriously. If you let your community know you're looking to expand your network and want to check out spaces that are outside of your circle, people will step up. I've done this before and have been connected to a network of pastors, a family-friendly Jewish/Pagan Shabbat, and a group of psychedelic-loving Hasidics. (No joke.) While all these communities are different, they're also examples of healthy congregations because they foster a sense of understanding and inclusion between participants.

Also subscribe to event lists for communities that might be a little out of your comfort zone. Personally, I'm subscribed to a lot of mailing lists for churches, healing centers, activist organizations, and art collectives. Just today a group called The People's Forum, which is a movement incubator for working class and marginalized communities, sent me an email that included a workshop called "Rhythm and Resilience." It dives into the theory and art of conga drums, and is taught by an activist, organizer and educator of Afro Puerto Rican Bomba, a traditional African-derived music and art form.

I signed up for the workshop twice.

In addition, going to events alone—especially the ones where you feel like you'll be uncomfortable—will lead to some of the most fascinating conversations of your life. Stepping into these situations will help you expand your understanding of your values and challenge your beliefs.

If you have social anxiety, or simply a fear of talking to strangers, this might sound impossible. So here's a hack: go into that interaction like you're already friends.

I stumbled upon this trick by accident. I was on my way to Mama Gena's "The Experience," a two-day gathering of women who want a sense of sisterhood and empowerment in their lives. The Javits Center in New York City was sold out, which meant a lot of ladies would be going there. Knowing that made my subway ride delightful. I looked around at the women around me, thinking, "She's a sister goddess." (That's what Mama Gena calls her students. You might roll your eyes, but it's playful as hell and I love it.)

Finally, seeing a group of women who were positively beaming, I popped the question: "Are you going to Mama Gena?"

It turns out, they weren't—but that started the conversation.

I was in such a good mood, and so sure we had something in common, that we ended up chatting for thirty minutes on the subway and swapping phone numbers. I even found out that Mama Gena's book, *Pussy*, was what convinced one of the women to quit her job and start her own business.

We bonded, and it was simply because I approached them with love.

A paper in the October, 2014 issue of the *Journal of Experimental Psychology: General* by Nick Epley and Juliana Schroeder did a study about interactions on public transit. One set of their field studies compared the enjoyment levels of commuters on trains and busses who engaged in conversation—or not. Members of a third group were given no instructions. Afterward, participants rated how much they enjoyed the commute as well as how productive they were.[33]

It turns out, the folks who had a conversation on public transit enjoyed their ride more than those who had been instructed not to engage with other people, as well as those in the control condition. At the same time, all participants rated themselves as about equally productive.[34]

So, what keeps us from talking to each other? Well, as a different study from the same scientists revealed, commuters think they are more interested in having people talk to them than other people are in being talked to. We avoid having conversations because we're afraid we're going to bother someone else. Yet at the same time, almost half of Americans wish they had more connection in their life. What gives?

The world needs more people who are willing to get uncomfortable in order to create a moment of connection. Let's be clear: talking to a stranger means you risk being rejected. And sure, it's scary, but it's time to embrace being scared. That's the only way to become un-lonely.

As Queen Oprah says, "The true meaning of courage is to be afraid, and then, with your knees knocking and your heart racing, to step out anyway."

KEY TAKEAWAYS

- It's easy to feel like we're the only ones with problems. Sharing with strangers is a way to feel connected to others, reduce shame around what we're dealing with, and remember that we're not alone.
- Sharing with strangers can allow us to speak more freely and learn new things about ourselves.
- Conversation agreements are key for creating a space where people feel safe to share.
- If you want to expand your social network, ask your community for help.

QUESTIONS TO CONSIDER

- How can we create more spaces that allow people to share their wisdom?

- What new opportunities can we create for people to connect with strangers?
- How can event organizers be encouraged to have more diverse leadership within their space?

5

SEEKING SPIRITUAL GUIDANCE

"Ideas spend eternity swirling around us, searching for available and willing human partners... When an idea thinks it has found somebody—say, you—who might be able to bring it into the world, the idea will pay you a visit... The idea will not leave you alone until it has your fullest attention. And then, in a quiet moment, it will ask, 'Do you want to work with me?'"

—ELIZABETH GILBERT

In December 2016, Katie Gordon experienced the exact ideological alchemy that Elizabeth Gilbert described. At the time, Katie was a student in Grand Rapids, Michigan.

The concept? To put nuns in a room with millennials who identify as a "none," AKA not religious. Katie believed this pairing would result in magic.

For all of this to make sense, it helps to backtrack a little.

Katie grew up in a Catholic household. Yet the theology never resonated with her, and she didn't feel like she was part of a community. So, when Katie was a teenager, she decided to leave the church.

Then in college, Katie's perspective on religion changed. She decided to go on a trip to India to work with a community development organization. "It was a pivotal moment in my religious life," Katie said. "I met Buddhists, Sikhs, Bahai, Hindus. People who I hadn't interacted with a lot before."

This trip led Katie to choose religion as her major— which resulted in her discovering interfaith dialogue. According to the United States of Peace Special Report, this practice is defined as "people of different religious faiths coming together to have a conversation." Those involved hope that the interactions will "unlock the power of religious traditions and provide the inspiration, guidance, and validation necessary for populations to move toward non-violent means of conflict resolution."[35]

As a result of her work as an interfaith leader, Katie started to meet nuns—also known as women religious. They just seemed like people whose lives were radically different from her own. Yet she never had an opportunity to sit down and chat with them.

That changed at a climate change march. Katie was walking toward the front and noticed that a group of Dominican sisters were leading the charge, holding a banner at the front.

They were starting to get tired. They'd been walking for hours. Being the kind soul that she is, Katie offered to take over. That's when she started a conversation with a sister. It turns out, the nun worked with The United Nations in New York City, recently attended the same human rights conference as Katie, and was passionate about social justice.

Katie was fascinated. The conversation completely countered her preconceptions about women religious. "I asked her if we could get coffee sometime," Katie said. After that, they kept meeting one-on-one.

These coffee dates meant the world to Katie. "She was genuinely curious and compassionate," she said. "She asked questions about my vocational and spiritual life. It was the most seen I'd felt by a religious leader. Honestly, it was the first time I felt like someone could accompany me on my spiritual journey."

I resonate with Katie's experience. In my years of attending congregational church, and going through confirmation myself, I never felt like I was learning about my spirituality. I never felt connected to a higher power, let alone the other people in my congregation. I had no sense of a "church family." Instead, it was a place where I was unwillingly dragged, grumbling the whole way, a few Sundays a month. I was not growing or being challenged. Instead, I felt like I was being held captive. Funny—a lot of the adults looked like that, too.

Like Katie, I didn't feel this sense of holy interconnection in organized religion. I felt it when I started bringing people together.

From where I'm standing, the worship of God or reverence for a pastor is not the most powerful part of church. Instead, it's the people standing in the pews next to me. That's where anyone can find the sacred, if they just turned their heads away from the cross and talked to their neighbors for longer than a simple "Peace be with you."

In healthy congregations, people feel seen and appreciated. They are reminded of the holiness that runs through their veins, rather than shamed for their sins. They buzz with the sense of aliveness that comes from connecting with other people and thinking about something outside of themselves.

Religious or otherwise, a healthy congregation is a vibrant and collaborative organism. Its members don't feel spoken down to. Rather, they're excited to grow with and learn from their leaders. There is a feeling that people are rising together and that they're connected to a higher purpose of helping each other. They feel more loved and less alone rather than ashamed of their shortcomings.

Unfortunately, a lot of people don't feel this way within organized religion. That's why they're leaving in higher numbers than ever before.

NUNS AND NONES

According to the Pew Research Center's Religious Landscape Study, 22.8 percent of Americans identify as "none," or religiously unaffiliated. Another 15.8 percent identify as "nothing in particular," and 1.5 percent are "other" faiths, which encompasses unitarians, humanists, pagans, Native American religions, "spiritual but not religious," and a few other groups. This makeup is far different than it was fifty years ago, when most people in the United States relied on a single religious community.

Yet just because someone attends church doesn't mean they get a sense of healthy congregation. The same Pew study found that one in five adults who attend church monthly or more say they do not usually feel God's presence; one in four don't usually feel a sense of community; and four in ten don't usually feel connected to their faith's history.

Katie felt this spiritual crisis while leading interfaith dialogues at multiple universities. "A lot of those people, from students to organizers, were also going through a spiritual crisis. So many people I met have a damaged relationship with the church," she said. "They were having the same challenges finding a spiritual community. So they wanted a space to have conversations to ask questions and share what we're thinking about."

That's when a brilliant solution popped into Katie's brain—bringing her friends and the nuns together.

And so, Nuns and Nones was born— a space for women religious and millennials without a religious affiliation to gather and learn from each other. There is no underlying agenda to convert the students. Instead, it's a gathering to talk about life's biggest questions. Being nuns, the women religious were more than equipped to handle that task.

"Nuns and Nones works because the sisters live into their tradition in a counter-cultural way," Katie said.

I had no idea how many women religious are oftentimes politically and socially radical. Like many people, my brain can only conjure an image of an angry lady slapping a kid's hand with a ruler. So, to redeem the nuns who have done some freakin' badass work, here's some background on these religious warriors:

Many of these women joined the covenant because they didn't want to get married, and wanted the opportunity to create a better world for all. As Cheryl L. Reed says in her book, *Unveiled: The Hidden Lives of Nuns*, «There's such a need for a community that cultivates women's spirituality and allows them to share in social justice mission with others.» She also estimates that around 70 percent of nuns are very feminist.[36]

It makes sense. In the 1940s and 50s, women's options were pretty much limited to getting married or being a nurse. As Reed says, religious life allowed women to step into» life outside of having a lot of kids and maybe being married to somebody you don't particularly like.»[37]

After the second Vatican counsel, nuns were freed from isolating themselves in worship. Instead, their role then was to go to the «root of their community,» and to discover their community's charism.

As Katie defines it, a charism is the spark of a community. It's their unique ministry, or what they're called to do. For example, the sisters of St. Joseph say that they are here for «unioning love,» AKA bringing people together in love and unity.

That is legitimately the most heart-warming definition of all time.

At first, people were unsure about Nuns and Nones, but curious enough to show up for a screening of a documentary called Radical Grace. It's about how three nuns, despite the Vatican reprimanding them for "radical feminism," follow their calling for social justice. One sister takes on Church patriarchy, another counsels former prisoners, and the third launches a cross-country Nuns on the Bus tour.[37]

Who knew that nuns were essentially action movie stars?

In one scene, Sister Simone Campbell breaks down on camera and cries with joy when she finds out that the Affordable Care Act is going to stay in place. In that moment, Katie realized how millennials and women religious could be allies in their work for progressive causes. As Katie told me, "We can learn a lot about social movements from Catholic sisters who've been doing this work for decades."

Adam Horowitz, one of the founders of Nuns and Nones, is part of a team that moved into a California convent for a six-month experiment in community living."I never thought that I'd be leading a shabbat in a convent," Adam told me. "I feel like we're all astronauts exploring a new planet." That's the risk of creating a different type of healthy congregation. Sometimes you don't know what you'll find, but the chance of bringing people together makes it worth it.

As of this writing, it's unclear what they will find. But I have a feeling it's going to be something good.

LOOKING FOR LEADERSHIP

When I was growing up in Fairfield, Connecticut, I didn't have many people in my life who I looked up to. Even though I lived an upper class life and was around people with plenty of privilege, I always got the sense that being a grownup sucked. After all, the dads I knew were stressed out from work. Most of the moms had a pervasive sense of sadness. In other words, many of the families I interacted with were highly dysfunctional. Most people around me weren't living with joy or vibrancy.

"Who are these people to tell me what to do when they seem miserable?" I thought. "Why should I listen to them?" I was desperate for someone to teach me how to create a happy life.

Turns out, I'm not alone in feeling this way. As a study conducted by the National Mentoring Partnership found, sixteen *million* young people in America—more than one in three—have never had an adult mentor of any kind.

In this study, a mentor is defined as "a supportive adult who works with a young person to build a relationship by offering guidance, support, and encouragement to help the young person's positive and healthy development over a period of time."

When surveyed, that same group of young people—sixteen million—said they wanted mentorship yet didn't know where to look for it. As a result, a large number of Americans are struggling to figure out how to make the transition into adulthood.[38]

It's interesting to consider that, no matter where these young people live, they are probably within the vicinity of a church, synagogue, or religious institution. Yet for whatever reason, they don't seek the guidance from a religious leader. Maybe they don't feel like they'll be welcomed. Perhaps they're afraid they'll be talked down to. Or maybe they're one of the increasing number of Americans who have no religion at all. On the other hand, these young people might have belonged to a faith but didn't see their congregation's leaders as a mentor.

Back in our more tribal days, it was okay if everyone wasn't equipped to pass down the wisdom of the ages. That's what the village shaman and storyteller was for! Yet now, a growing number of young Americans have no idea where to learn how to live a happy and fulfilled life. Many parents, even though they're doing their best, don't have the tools to help their child thrive.

This makes me wonder: who is our go-to person for life's big questions? Are we simply supposed to go it alone, without anyone to guide us along our paths?

This dilemma is explained perfectly in "Care of Souls," a report created by Harvard Divinity School's How We Gather program:

"Fifty years ago, most people in the United States relied on a single religious community to conduct spiritual practices, ritualize life moments, foster healing, connect to lineage, inspire morality, house transcendent experience, mark holidays, support family, serve the needy, work for justice, and—through art, song, text, and speech—tell and retell a

common story to bind them together. Now, we might rely on the Insight Meditation Timer, mountain hikes, Afro-Flow Yoga, Instagram hashtags, Friday shabbatlucks, Beyoncé anthems, and protesting the Muslim Ban. But no common story.

"As we've unbundled and remixed, we've also isolated and made insecure. If I write my gratitude journal alone and whisper a prayer in the shower, am I doing it right? Will I offend my friend with the text I send after her mother dies? With no collective place to share our deep sorrows and joys, they begin to feel illegitimate. And this is exactly what we have to relegitimize: binding ourselves together in our deepest experience of being human. It's time to turn to the Care of Souls."

That passage connects to both the deep desire that I had for community growing up, as well as my total bewilderment over where to get that need met.

The authors of this report—Angie, Casper, and Sue—suggest there is a solution to "today's social and spiritual disconnection." It is an emerging field, called the Care of Souls, which applies ancient wisdom to modern problems. This caring for others will be the solution to loneliness and a lack of purpose.

In their report, the team offers seven key roles in the caring of souls: Gatherer, Seer, Maker, Healer, Venturer, Steward, and—notable for this chapter—the Elder. This role gives weight to the older folks in our society who are so often cast aside. In the report, they define elders as people who "ground our gifts in history and community." Yet while their role is necessary, they are often forgotten. The HDS team describes this problem eloquently:

"How can Elders call forth gifts in community, without community? Once rooted in extended families and religious congregations, Elders have been largely displaced by geographic mobility and religious disaffiliation. In white culture especially, the disease of disconnection devalues people as they age. But even in communities with stronger legacies of eldering, erosion is underway. Thousands of potential Elders are isolated, unable to bestow their wisdom to emerging leaders and communities in dire need of it."

The first time I read that passage, I let out a long breath. It hit me hard. "How many problems could we avoid if we simply listened to the people who have been through these things before?" I wondered. "What would happen if we raised the elderly up for their knowledge rather than hiding them away because we see them as useless and out of touch?"[40]

If you don't believe ageism is rampant in the professional world, consider this: there is a week-long retreat in Mexico, called Modern Elder Academy, for Silicon Valley employees who are struggling to come to grips with their age. Believe it or not, most of their attendees are in their thirties and forties.[41] While that's not old in the slightest, these workers feel like they're becoming old hat very quickly. They understand that, in an industry that relies on constant innovation and values youthful energy, their perceived worth dwindles as they age.

Anthropologist and explorer, Elizabeth Kapu'uwailani Lindsey, says, "I believe that when an elder dies, a library is burned: vast sums of wisdom and knowledge are lost. Throughout the world libraries are ablaze with scant attention."[42]

In a healthy congregation, we invite the elderly into our gatherings and welcome the opportunity to learn from their wisdom. One of these missed exchanges is like a single burning page. Yet when our entire culture is designed to ignore the voices of the elderly and celebrate young people, that lost knowledge is the equivalent of an entire library on fire.

THREE SHIFTS FOR WISDOM SEEKING

After many conversations with spiritual leaders, Joy List subscribers, and space makers, I've discovered three major ways we can increase our ease of access to mentorship, both in terms of spiritual guidance and advice in general.

While these are by no means the only changes that need to take place in order to reestablish the importance of eldership and provide people with the wisdom that they crave, they're a good first step:

1) CREATE AND PROMOTE INTERGENERATIONAL SPACES

We need more spaces in society where all generations can have meaningful interactions with each other. This can be done through mentorship, spiritual guidance, or even community projects. When done right, each generation benefits from the interactions and helps cement the idea of healthy congregation within all levels of the community. As Douglas Massey writes in *Strangers in a Strange Land*, "The farther apart two groups are on a social dimension, the greater their spatial separation in the urban landscape."[8] We need to fix this.

I see this firsthand in New York City, a place that's known as America's melting pot—yet people from different generations are rarely together. The age range of most events I've attended is twenty-two to thirty-five. There aren't any children or older people. This results in our perception of the world being seen through our own narrow lens. It would be blown open simply by the wonder of a child or the wisdom of an elder.

At one of my recent Joy List Socials—an event where you can show up by yourself and leave with a new friend—we opened with a dance workshop. A lot of the people who attended were noticeably nervous. They weren't used to being in dance spaces, and the tension showed up in their body language. I worried that the awkwardness would stifle our freedom of movement.

Yet then, something wonderful happened. A woman walked in with her four-year-old daughter. The little girl immediately started running around the room and through people's legs, giggling the whole time. Her high energy and silliness completely opened up the room. It was like a pressure valve had been released. People's shoulders relaxed and their eyes began to smile. No one can continue to act like they're too cool when they're doing the twist with a four-year-old!

Organizations like Generations United, which creates intergenerational policies and programs, have been created to help both the young and the elderly learn from one another. Yet even though they reach thousands of people, the fact remains that most Americans aren't touched by the group.

That leaves us with the question: how can we stop the growing gap between generations? How can we give every generation the respect it deserves?

2) MODEL NEW FORMS OF SPIRITUAL LEADERSHIP

People attend religious services for many reasons. Most of them are listed below, as found in a study conducted by the Pew Research Center:

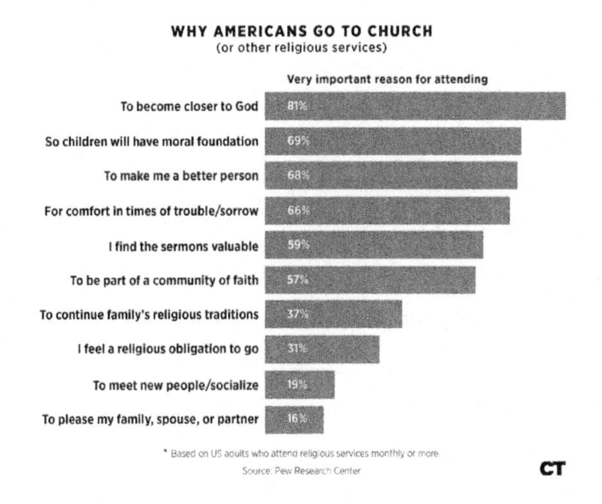

Unfortunately, these needs aren't being met by most services. As I mentioned earlier in the book, one in five adults who attend church monthly or more say they do not usually feel God's presence. One in four don't usually feel a sense of community. Four in ten don't usually feel connected to their faith's history.[43]

In other words, even the people who attend church don't feel connected to God. Clearly, organized religion needs an overhaul.

Lab/Shul, a self-proclaimed God-optional, everybody-friendly version of Judaism in New York City, does exactly that.

I recently attended one of their Sabbaths, and was struck by how different it was from any other service I'd been to. First of all, they had done an amazing job of bringing people together from different generations: families, older couples, and young professionals alike.

I volunteered to check people in and was struck by how many folks said, "I'm a regular." They came with treats for the snack table as well as an abundance of hugs to give. As a greeter, I was on the lookout for newcomers who were standing on the outskirts of conversations. Yet the frequent flyers did a great job assimilating them, and soon the whole room was buzzing with happy discussions.

And then, the actual service started. In the center of the room was a circle of chairs, each filled with a musician. There was a guitarist, a drummer, and multiple singers. Frankly, I couldn't stop staring at them. They all glowed with happiness, playing a song and making jokes with each other as we found our seats. "That's what deeply belonging in a community looks like," I thought as I sat next to my new friend, a fellow greeter.

Throughout the evening, the group sang a number of songs in Hebrew and English. Even though I'm not Jewish, they were easy enough to pick up—and all of the words were displayed on a screen. At one point, a woman sang an original song that was hauntingly beautiful. The room sat in silence until the drum began to pick up, and the room began to raise their voices in another song.

Between musical interludes, the rabbi talked about the meaning of Sabbath—disconnecting from the world and resting, even though there is still work to be done. That night, the government was teetering on the edge of shutdown. I was impressed that the rabbi mentioned it. Later, I learned that Lab/Shul regularly brings conversations about social justice into their services.

Throughout the evening there were references to paganism, queerness, the patriarchy, and white supremacy. Some of the songs were very sensual and had mentions of sexuality. In other words, it was everything that was completely removed from my church experience growing up.

I was hooked.

At the end of the night, I learned that Lab/Shul would be doing a "Soul Spa," AKA a Sabbath, at House of Yes—the club that regularly hosts my favorite dance party, The Get Down. I couldn't believe it. A Jewish get-together... in a club? Of course, I immediately volunteered for glitter application duty.

As Peter Block says in *Community*, "Community building requires a concept of the leader as one who creates experiences for others—experiences that in themselves are examples of our desired future."[45]

The team at Lab/Shul creates a real life example of a religious experience that is genuinely "everyone-friendly." I'm not Jewish, and I still go occasionally. In my opinion, they are achieving the primary goal—and most failed objective—of organized religion: to help people feel closer to God and each other. People worship to be better people, find comfort, and gain a sense of community. A healthy congregation can accomplish the same things.

Of course, many people still don't feel comfortable entering an organized religious service at all. They might be an atheist, or simply had a bad experience at a service growing up and don't want to go back. That's why it's important for people to create consistent healthy congregations, which include the other ways to foster belonging that are mentioned throughout this book.

3) CREATE COMMUNITY HUBS

Our neighbors have a lot to teach us. So when we're isolated for too long, we don't just prevent ourselves from feeling connected. We also keep ourselves from learning. Yet at the same time, it's hard to ask for help with loneliness. As I've mentioned before, it's a stigmatized feeling. That's exactly why community centers are so important. They're a natural space for people to connect without the awkwardness that might come from an online date or networking event.

At the moment, community centers are not super popular in America. Even in New York City, there aren't many free spaces where you can meet people and relax for an extended period of time. Coffee shops and coworking spaces simply don't have the right atmosphere. Even the YMCA has become more of a center for workshops than a space to make new friends.

In other countries, the government is experimenting with spaces that bring people together. Australia, for example, has taken an unorthodox approach—sheds.

Men's Sheds is a social program that provides community spaces for men to boost their emotional and physical health.

These spaces provide a haven for men to make things with their hands and meet other men who are passionate about sharing skills. It also helps reduce loneliness, which is especially prevalent amongst retired men. As Age UK found in a study, one of their primary activities is watching television, which is not exactly a soul-filling activity. That's where sheds come in.

According to a study by Manchester Metropolitan University, these hubs have created a sense of camaraderie and belonging for men. As one attendee said in an article for The Conversation, "It saved me from an early grave … I was in a right state and this was good for me." This man was literally suicidal, and sharing conversation around woodworking saved his life. If that doesn't prove the life-changing power of wisdom exchange, I don't know what will.

While the project started in Australia in 1998, it now has hundreds of sheds around the world.[44] Yet while this effort has made a huge impact, hundreds of others will need to be created in order to deal with the global epidemic of loneliness.

* * *

Peter Block says in his book, *Community*, "Have a conversation that we have not had before, one that has the power to create something new in the world."[45]

When it comes to the transformation of organized religion, a lot of conversations aren't happening. Fewer people are attending religious services, yet alternative gatherings for spiritual life are slow to appear. Young people are desperate for mentorship, but often do not trust traditional religious leaders. In order to keep America's spiritual life alive, we need to uplift the people who are doing the work to create gatherings that feel sacred—especially those who have decades of experience under their belts. Mentorship needs to be encouraged between the young and the old, and community hubs need to be created to bring people together from all walks of life. Otherwise, loneliness will skyrocket even more, exacerbated by a disconnection from our neighbors and a sense of something that's bigger than ourselves.

KEY TAKEAWAYS

- Even if you're not religious, it's still helpful to have guidance from an elder figure. These intergenerational relationships are important and becoming increasingly rare in America.
- Finding or creating a healthy congregation, even if it has nothing to do with religion, is necessary for feeling like you're a part of something bigger than you.

- Three effective ways to promote mentorship are creating intergenerational spaces, modeling new forms of spiritual leadership, and creating community hubs.

QUESTIONS TO CONSIDER

- How can we invest in more centers that foster a sense of community, especially intergenerationally?
- What can we do to save convents and ensure that they're still being used for social justice work?
- What does the new community center look like? How can it reduce loneliness?

6

FINDING HEALING SPACES

"One thing: you have to walk and create the way by you're walking; you will not find a ready-made path. It is not so cheap, to reach to the ultimate realization of truth. You will have to create the path by walking yourself; the path is not ready-made, lying there and waiting for you. It is just like the sky: the birds fly, but they don't leave any footprints. You cannot follow them; there are no footprints left behind."

—OSHO

I'm staring into a mirror, tears streaming down my face. My eyes are puffy, my face is red, and my body is shaking slightly. "What do you see?" asks Erika, a facilitator who stands behind me with a hand gently resting on my shoulder. I pause for a moment, my breath sharp from crying so heavily.

"I see someone who is in pain," I tell her. "I see someone who needs to let it out."

"Good," Erika says. "What else do you need to let out?" She removes the mirror, revealing a woman who is sitting across from me in a folding chair. I have chosen her to be the stand-in for my father. Taking a deep breath, I let out a torrent of angry words. I don't stop for five whole minutes.

Eventually, I pause. I take a deep breath. The feeling of sadness has gone and is replaced by rage. In this moment, one of the facilitators hands me a pillow. "What do you want to do with it?" she asks. A little unsure, I shakily hand the pillow to my pretend dad. Erika grins. "What do you *really* want to do?" she asks, smiling.

This time, I know what I need. I take the pillow, hold it over my head, and throw it across the room as hard as I can. As I do, I let out a deep, guttural scream—a sound I've never heard come out of my body before. Immediately, I'm handed another pillow. "Again," someone says encouragingly. So I do it again, even louder and more primal this time. I feel like an animal who has finally been released from its cage, and has something to say about how long it's been cooped up.

I stand there, shaking, and look to my left. A room of twenty women are sitting, cross-legged, silently bearing witness to my healing. In the heat of the moment, I'd completely forgotten they were there. But I'm glad they were.

Before I can get too self-conscious, the mirror is put back in front of me. "What do you see now?" Erika asks. I look at myself, eyes wild and face flushed. I push my shoulders back and grin. "I see someone who is absolutely beautiful," I announce to the room. "I see someone who has suffered and is ready to heal. I see a woman, not a girl."

With those words, a pile of tension is released from my body. At this point, I know my work is done.

This moment is a scene from Woman Within, a three-day weekend for female-identifying folks who want to recover from trauma, deeply feel their emotions, and get in touch with—you guessed it—the woman within. Out of all the retreats I've done, and there have been many, this was the most emotionally taxing. For seventy-two hours I was given the gift of witnessing women heal from the type of tragedy that almost never comes up in conversation.

Together, we held space for each other's stories. We listened. We cried. And at the end of the weekend, despite all of the pain we moved through, we danced. We went through hell and back together—and then boogied our faces off because, after all that shit, we're still alive.

Every person on this planet has experienced trauma. Unfortunately, most of us don't have a space to properly process the experience. As a result, those feelings fester inside our bodies. We hold our pain inside, thinking we're the only ones who hurt this much. We shy away from dealing with the pain because we worry it will encompass us and we will never escape.

Healthy congregations create space for healing. They help people feel safe enough to access their pain, and learn that others have survived similar hardships. Healthy congregations don't just talk about the good feelings in life. They embrace heaviness and allow members to face their suffering head on. After all, the only way out of pain is to move through it.

The world needs more healing spaces. In this chapter I'll dig a little deeper into why they matter and then explain how you can find and create your own. Places to deal with trauma are truly sacred, and there aren't nearly enough of them. From men's circle leaders to Alcoholics Anonymous facilitators, I celebrate everyone who brings people together to touch their pain. When we can feel less alone in our struggle, we heal.

MOVING THROUGH PAIN TOGETHER

Warning: this chapter is about to get pretty freakin' heavy. If you're not in the headspace for that, move onto "Developing Rituals." Otherwise, buckle up and get ready to feel some feels.

The term "healing spaces" is pretty vague. What types of wounds am I actually talking about here? What does "healing" even look like? Well, after lots of trial and error, I've attempted to create a basic definition for the phrase.

Healing spaces allow someone to shakily expose the most vulnerable parts of themselves and be met with love. They are safe places for them to bring awareness to the suffering they often try to keep at bay. These spaces allow them to feel their pain in the presence of others, which simultaneously helps them feel less burdened and more supported.

Yet what types of wounds am I actually talking about here? What would someone need to heal from? It's not like everyone is walking around with a deep, dark secret locked inside of them, right?

Well, here's the thing. A lot of people are.

In the seminal text about trauma, *The Body Keeps the Score*, Bessel van der Kolk, M.D., labels child abuse as our nation's largest public health problem.[46]

Let that sink in for a minute. How many conversations have you heard about obesity, heart disease, and cancer? Then consider how many discussions you've been involved in about child abuse. Probably close to zero.

Child abuse and loneliness have a big thing in common. There is a stigma around talking about them. As a result, everyone thinks they're one of the few people dealing with it. Yet in reality, both experiences are far more common than the public dialogue would suggest.

If we didn't hold shame around our feelings of isolation and experiences of abuse, we could truly start making a change. Yet discussions of child abuse, even more than loneliness, are swept under the rug. If we pretend it doesn't exist, we don't have to deal with it... right?

Unfortunately, 1 in 4 girls and 1 in 6 boys will be assaulted before they reach adulthood. Far more experience emotional and physical abuse.[47]

As van der Kolk notes in his book, a vastly underreported study from the CDC, called the Adverse Childhood Experiences (ACE) Study, revealed that the overall costs of child abuse "exceeded those of cancer or heart disease and that eradicating child abuse in America would reduce the overall rate of depression by more than half, alcoholism by two-thirds, and suicide, IV drug use, and domestic violence by three-quarters. It would also have a dramatic effect on workplace performance and vastly decrease the need for incarceration."[48]

How is this possible? Well, abuse is considered an adverse childhood experience. The CDC's ACE Study confirmed that there is a direct link between childhood trauma and the chronic diseases people develop as adults, as well as social and emotional problems. This includes heart disease, lung cancer, diabetes, autoimmune diseases, depression, violence, being a victim of violence, and suicide.

An ACE score essentially predicts someone's risk for disease based on childhood stress.

At this point, you probably having a sinking feeling in your stomach and are wondering what your own ACE score is. You can find out using the questions below. If you're not in a positive headspace, this is an activity you should hold off on until you're feeling more stable.

Prior to your eighteenth birthday:

1. Did a parent or other adult in the household often or very often... Swear at you, insult you, put you down, or humiliate you? or Act in a way that made

you afraid that you might be physically hurt? No___If Yes, enter 1 ___

2. Did a parent or other adult in the household often or very often... Push, grab, slap, or throw something at you? or Ever hit you so hard you had marks or were injured? No ___ If Yes, enter 1 ___
3. Did an adult or person at least five years older than you ever... Touch or fondle you or have you touch their body in a sexual way? or Attempt or actually have oral, anal, or vaginal intercourse with you? No ___If Yes, enter 1 ___
4. Did you often or very often feel that ... No one in your family loved you or thought you were important or special? or Your family didn't look out for each other, feel close to each other, or support each other? No ___ If Yes, enter 1 ___
5. Did you often or very often feel that ... You didn't have enough to eat, had to wear dirty clothes, and had no one to protect you? or Your parents were too drunk or high to take care of you or take you to the doctor if you needed it? No ___If Yes, enter 1 ___
6. Were your parents ever separated or divorced? No ___If Yes, enter 1 ___
7. Was your mother or stepmother: Often or very often pushed, grabbed, slapped, or had something thrown at her? or Sometimes, often, or very often

kicked, bitten, hit with a fist, or hit with something hard? or Ever repeatedly hit over at least a few minutes or threatened with a gun or knife?
No ___ If Yes, enter 1 ___

8. Did you live with anyone who was a problem drinker or alcoholic, or who used street drugs?
No ___ If Yes, enter 1 ___
9. Was a household member depressed or mentally ill, or did a household member attempt suicide?
No ___ If Yes, enter 1 ___
10. Did a household member go to prison?
No ___ If Yes, enter 1 ___

Now add up your "Yes" answers: ___. This is your ACE Score.

Know this: no matter what your score is, each of these experiences is something that needs to be actively processed as an adult. For example, maybe none of these apply except for the fact that you never felt supported as a child. This is something that you still need to look at head-on, or it will impact your physical and mental health, as well as your relationships. Below is a graph, which shows how many ACEs the study's population had, broken up in terms of percentage between men and women.[47]

Number of Adverse Childhood Experiences (ACE Score)	Women	Men	Total
0	34.5	38.0	36.1
1	24.5	27.9	26.0
2	15.5	16.4	15.9
3	10.3	8.6	9.5
4 or more	15.2	9.2	12.5

Many health studies primarily use inner-city poor people of color as their test subjects. However, the study's participants were 17,000 mostly white, middle and upper-middle class college-educated San Diegans with good jobs and great health care. They all belonged to the Kaiser Permanente health maintenance organization. I highlight this to show that childhood trauma is very common, even with employed white middle-class, college-educated people who have great health insurance.

At this point, you might be freaking out a little. But before you have a full-blown panic attack, know that childhood trauma is not a life sentence. There are ways for you to improve your resilience and live a happy and healthy life as an adult. As a study from Interface Children Family Services states, having good friends who are there when we need them, practicing mindfulness, and helping others can all contribute to making a person more resilient. Healthy congregations, and especially those that include healing spaces, allow for all of that to happen.[48]

Unaddressed trauma is one of the reasons why so many people feel deeply disconnected. They don't have a safe space to process those painful emotions. As a result, it's easier to push people away than to bring them in close. Thankfully, some facilitators are skilled enough to create a safe space for this type of vulnerable connection. Their healing spaces allow you to feel secure enough to create healthier relationships that allow intimacy. These remind you that you're not alone.

RITUAL FOR HEALING

It was a chilly Friday night in October, and I had no plans. I was about to text my friend Duncan when, no surprise, I get a group text from the very same man. "Crew!" he said. "Going to see this amazing documentary about a men's group in Folsom Prison called *The Work*. Opening weekend. Let's go support!"

Two hours later and I was sliding into my seat in a half-filled movie theater.

The first moment of the film is a low, guttural chant: "Zim-bah-way." It's being bellowed out by James McLeary, a large black man wearing a yarmulke, who stands in the center of a circle of men. Every time he finishes one call, the rest of the group responds with a noise that comes deep from their belly: "Shoo!" The sound sends a chill up my spine.

For the next ninety minutes, I am more gripped by a film than I have ever been in my entire life.

The Work is an inside look at a men's group inside of Folsom Prison. Half of the participants are prisoners; half are men from the outside. The cameramen sit within the group circles, which gives viewers a painfully intimate look into the process of men who are working through decades of emotions they have been forced to stuff away. As you can imagine, it's not pretty when the layers begin to peel away.[49]

In one electric moment of the film, a man realizes he's been holding something in that he needs to say to his dad. Immediately a facilitator asks him to pick someone in the group to serve as a representation. Once chosen, that symbolic father figure stood on the outside of the circle. The rest of the group surrounded the man, asking him what he wanted to say to his father. They pushed the person in the center, telling him that he wasn't a real man, until his anger finally starts to boil. He begins pushing against the arms of the men and screaming: "Why won't you spend time with me? Why won't you spend time with me?" Again and again, he throws himself against a wall of men.

Finally, he collapses. His body relaxes, and a smile crosses his face. Something has been released.

As Gethin, the film's director, later told me:

"You'll never feel a container like that one. It's electric. You can touch it. There's magic, and it's hard to put your finger on. Yet I've just had too many experiences where I've seen a man transform and thought, 'This is impossible.' And that kind of change can happen because we really take the time to set the space. We make it safe. There's poetry. There's chanting. Plus, the men in prison are really fucking committed. They know this matters, and they only have three or four days. Then they're done. They've got to put their armor back on and go back into the world of Folsom."

When the credits have rolled and the lights go up, the entire theater is dead silent. My body is covered in goosebumps.

At that moment, some of the crew from the film are there to take questions. One of them is the man who led the chant!

Finally, a woman raises her hand. "Can you do the chant with us?" she asks. "Yes!" I call out, grinning. There's a pause, and I worry that I offended him. Thankfully, he looks at us both, smiles, and stands taller. "Alright," he says. "Everyone stand."

Immediately, the entire theater rises as he calls out the first "Zim-bah-way." It reverberates throughout the theater. We answer back: "Shoo!" He calls again. We respond. Faster and faster we chant, until he finally puts his hand up, signaling us to stop. The room quiets, and the air feels electric.

Because of that screening, both Duncan and I felt connected to Gethin. We wanted to supported him however we could—and to become his friends. That's how I ended up sitting with Gethin in a coffee shop, asking him how he got started in the world of men's work in the first place.

It turns out, Gethin used to think group therapy was bullshit. In fact, when one of his friends invited him to The Mankind Project—a facilitated retreat for men to process emotions and discuss masculinity—he completely ignored him. Yet his friend was determined. Every time he saw Gethin, he would ask, "Have you done it yet?" And every time, for six years, Gethin responded with a "Fuck off!"

Sometime during the seventh year, Gethin couldn't sleep. He was tossing and turning in bed, staring at the ceiling. Then, out of the blue, a thought popped into his brain: "That Mankind thing my friend keeps telling me about? I need it, and I need it now."

All Gethin knew about The Mankind Project was that it gave men an initiation ritual into manhood. According to his friend, it helped men leave behind their childhood and step into who they truly are. That used to sound stupid to Gethin. He didn't understand why diving into childhood wounds would be helpful, or why these guys felt like they weren't truly in their "manhood."

But, for some reason, something had shifted in him. He realized something was missing in his life, but he couldn't figure out what it was. Yet he was confident that he was going to find it through Mankind Project.

The next morning Gethin called his local Mankind Project chapter and found out they were hosting something called "The New Warrior Project" in a little over a week. Without even hesitating, he signed up.

I asked Gethin what he needed from that experience. After pausing for a moment, he said, "I knew I needed to shed something in order to step into manhood. Rituals for that don't exist in our society anymore."

Looking back twelve years later, Gethin realized that he started healing from his childhood during that weekend. "I wouldn't say I had the worst childhood," he told me. "But there were things I'd picked up along the way that I needed to put down." He also felt like he tapped back into a sense of inner knowing that he'd lost through the years. "Thanks to The Mankind Project, my inner voice, or my inner intelligence, came back. I've learned to trust it and hear what's right and when I'm faking things."

Men's work is so transformative for Gethin that he still goes to a private weekly men's circle, called an "I group."

One moment in his years with these men really stands out to Gethin. They were doing some work and something bothered him. "I can't even remember what it was," Gethin remembered. "I was just sitting in my chair, kind of rocking. And I told the guys, 'I just to want to fall on the floor.'"

With that, one of them looked him dead in the eyes and asked, "So, why don't you?"

So, surrounded by men who he trusted completely, Gethin got on the ground.

"I just fell on the floor like I was eight years old, feeling terrified," Gethin said. "In that moment, the little boy in me was feeling unseen and unheld. Something at work had triggered it, and I needed to recognize that. And I needed to let it go. The other men around me just witnessed it, and it felt amazing. That helped me realize and express the part of me that just wanted to curl up and hide because I'd been hurt."

Gethin told me that his group is like church for him, with a small difference. "The problem with religion is guilt. Original sin. Sometimes I come to group and I'm uncomfortable. I'm in a bad mood. But I show up, and all of me is welcome."

SPACE TO BE

Finding an affinity group—AKA a group of people with the same background as you in one way or another—is not frequent on the "Ten Top Self-Care Tips" listicles that abound on the Internet. Yet seeking out these spaces is one of the best things that you can do for your sense of belonging. In a world that can be truly exhausting, it's okay to seek out environments that are intentionally safe. In fact, it's necessary for healing.

Being in a place where you don't have to explain yourself is truly regenerative. It's an opportunity to let your shoulders relax, feel the love of others, and forget about whatever ways you are "other." Here, your otherness makes you at home.

Jeanine T. Abraham, an African-American actress who leads Urban JourneyDance—a healing movement-based immersive theatre workshop in Brooklyn—was reminded of this when she ran a workshop at a wellness center in upstate New York. All of the women on the retreat were white.

People told Jeanine over the course of the weekend how beautifully she moved. They said she looked exotic and attempted to copy her rhythm. In the moment, Jeanine would just smile and say, "Thank you." Yet if she had the energy, she would say something different.

"At a lot of 'conscious dance' retreats, it feels like white women process their guilt through me," Jeanine told me. "When I dance, I heal and I feel free. The longer I danced in white spaces the harder it became. I felt like I was being objectified by the white people in the room, who felt comfortable co-opting my healing for themselves. It was like being naked in public for someone else's pleasure. My healing was on display. I found myself going home feeling exhausted, depleted from taking on a lot of other people's energy."

For a long time, Jeanine was facilitating JourneyDance in New York City. Yet she never felt at home in their facilitator community. "I was always one of the only people of color," Jeanine explained. "People saw what I was doing, and they tried to appropriate my energy. They would come to my workshops, only to ask me to teach them how to do what I do, to give them my playlists without ever offering to pay me anything, ever."

Jeanine was helping others heal but didn't have a space to heal herself. Understandably, she left the JourneyDance community for a while.

Around the same time, Jeanine also lost her apartment to gentrification in New York City... and was broken up with... and had to occasionally stay with her parents. Needless to say, it was a low point.

And then, Jeanine got an email with this subject line: "You're going to the mountain top."

The message was sent from a nonprofit called GirlTrek. Jeanine Googled them and was immediately inspired by their message. As their homepage states, "In the footsteps of a civil rights legacy, GirlTrek is a national health movement that activates thousands of Black women to be change makers in their lives and communities—through walking."

Once a year, GirlTrek has a Summit where they train black women how to practice self-care—beginning with walking thirty minutes a day. They also learn how to be in nature and organize the GirlTrek movement in their own community. It turns out, the founders had been following Jeanine's online presence and were inspired by her open heart and unstoppable spirit.

"They told me, in no uncertain terms, that I was coming to the training as a facilitator," Jeanine said. "They wanted me to lead JourneyDance."

At the time, Jeanine thought no one was watching her dance videos, which she was posting on YouTube. She had no idea that one of the cofounders of GirlTrek, Vanessa, had been following her journey for six years.

"That experience helped me realize that I never know who's watching my art," Jeanine said. "And that I just need to keep doing what lights me up."

Vanessa wasn't taking no for an answer, so Jeanine said, "Yes."

Since she had never been to an organizer training, Jeanine had no idea what to expect. She was about to enter a space filled with 150 women she had never met and facilitate a JourneyDance she created specifically for black women for the first time.

At the time, Jeanine was nervous. Yet looking back, it was one of the most renewing experiences of her life.

"Dancing with black women is liberating," Jeanine said. "I see my ancestors reflected in their movement. It's like I'm finally home."

One moment in particular stands out to Jeanine—dancing with an eighteen-year-old girl. They were moving together, singing and smiling. Some of the songs were more recent, which made the younger woman light up. Others were favorites of Jeanine's, and her enthusiasm would pass on to the teenager. Throughout it all, they shared movement. No words were spoken.

"It was this beautiful moment when I felt like I was passing on a tradition," Jeanine said, tearing up. "I truly believe enslaved Africans trapped on slave ships used their imaginations and dance rituals to get out of their heads and survive. Today African-Americans still utilize the power of music, dance and theatre to process our trauma. It's really powerful."

By the end of both ten-day trainings, Jeanine finally felt like she had an authentic support system. For the first time, she wasn't one of the few people of color in a yoga studio or a dance room. She was surrounded by people who understood her and weren't trying to appropriate her.

The organizer training has become so popular that GirlTrek created the Stress Protest Labor Day weekend retreat in Colorado. In 2019, one thousand women are expected to attend. Also inspired by those trainings, GirlTrek received one of the first TED innovator grants and created a twenty-three-city wellness revival tour as a free wellness retreat and organizer training for black women in America's most marginalized black communities. GirlTrek has invited Jeanine to every event as their movement motivator and pays her a fair living wage for her talents.

"I've found that 'white guilt' can prevent black people and white people from being in authentic relationship with each other," Jeanine said. "There's this element of having to constantly have to educate or coddle white friends, which makes it harder to grow trust. I now know that black people and white people need the freedom to do our healing work in our own spaces, to ground ourselves. Then, we can come together interracially with a solid foundation."

WHAT CREATES A HEALING SPACE?

There's something about Gethin's circle and Jeanine's JourneyDance that allows them to feel safe enough to be vulnerable. It shares the same qualities of many other healing spaces, which create the container for people to heal in community. These gatherings are truly some of the most powerful things a space-maker can create. While it takes a confident facilitator to hold space for this work, the world needs more people who are willing to fill that role.

To make this vulnerable space possible, there needs to be a few foundational elements in place:

1) Skilled facilitation: I could drop my walls and bawl my eyes out at Woman Within because I trusted the facilitators. I knew they had been through multiple trainings in order to be a supportive presence for me. In fact, one of the women who was coaching me through my work had staffed the weekend over forty times.

I also trusted the facilitators because they were vulnerable with the participants of the weekend. At the start of the experience, each of them shared what had brought them to the Woman Within program in the first place. Unsurprisingly, they had all suffered from some sort of trauma. The weekend was so helpful for them that they wanted to give the same opportunity to other women. That's why they were there.

These women were not pretending to be all-powerful healers who had all the answers. Instead, they trusted us enough to expose the raw parts of themselves. This allowed me to feel more comfortable being vulnerable with them.

2) Clear intention: Is there anything more awkward than being dragged to a fundraiser by a friend, only to realize you have no idea what you're showing up for? Yeah. It's difficult to feel connected to people when you don't know what you have in common. Yet if your common values are clear, bonds can be formed more easily.

At Woman Within, we all knew we were there for healing. We understood that no one there thought they were just in for a chill vacation, or a fun few days filled with gossip and margaritas. From the start, it was clear that our intention was to do soul work. This helped me feel in solidarity with the other women in the group. I knew they were the type of people who would dedicate a weekend to doing some pretty difficult work to improve their lives. This not only helped me feel supported but also made me want to support them.

3) **Setting the space:** Even a few small gestures can let your attendees know that you thought about them before they entered the room. This can do wonders for people who feel anxious, and let them know they're cared for. This can be as simple as cleaning and putting out some snacks to burning palo santo—a sacred clearing wood—to cleanse the space of any negative energy. Even if you're sitting in the cafeteria of an elementary school, a circle of chairs feels a little more special when there's a candle and some beautiful stones set out in the middle. By making these small gestures, you are creating sacred space.

4) **Opening and closing ritual:** Ritual takes the mundane and makes it magical. It takes a few people sitting together in the room and makes the gathering feel sacred. Ritual is a signal that says, "What we are doing here is important. We are conscious of these simple actions, and they are powerful."

The Woman Within weekend started with a group conversation about why we were there and how the staff would guide us through the weekend. We sang and meditated and journaled together. From that moment, it was clear we were in for a journey and this was an intentional space. On the same token, the weekend closed with us dancing, singing, and playing the drums. We concluded the experience with a ritual that women have been doing together throughout time. It felt primal. It also wrapped the gathering up on a positive note, which is pretty extraordinary considering the heaviness of the weekend. These rituals signaled that a healing journey was about to start or end, which allowed me to be fully present. Examples of ritual will be covered in the next chapter.

5) **Full participation:** A healing space loses its power when someone doesn't want to be there or doesn't buy in to the purpose of the gathering. Even if everyone else is totally enthusiastic, one person questioning the validity of the space is enough to make somebody else think, "Wait? Is this stupid? Should I even be here?" That single wet blanket can dampen the atmosphere for everyone.

To be clear, full participation does not always mean that everyone needs to be actively sharing. Simply sitting and listening can be immensely healing for both the individual and the group. After all, being heard is transformative. I personally went to three Adult Children of Alcoholics meetings before I even dared to open my mouth and speak. Yet hearing the stories of other people and realizing I was not alone in my struggle was immensely helpful. At the same time, I felt at ease because I knew I didn't have to join the conversation. The best healing spaces make room for people who are prepared to share and those who are only ready to listen.

KEY TAKEAWAYS

- Adverse childhood experiences impact us long into adulthood. We need healing spaces to process this trauma and build the resiliency to have a healthy life.
- Sometimes you need to be in spaces with people who understand what you've been through.
- Healing spaces should only be created by skilled facilitators.

QUESTIONS TO CONSIDER

- How can we promote the work of the best healing spaces and make them more widely accessible?
- What programs can be developed to give a large audience the skills to help others heal from trauma and become more resilient?
- Who can provide the funds to facilitators who want to lead healing spaces but don't have the financial means to do so?

7

INCORPORATING RITUAL

"We do spiritual ceremonies as human beings in order to create a safe resting place for our most complicated feelings of joy or trauma, so that we don't have to haul those feelings around with us forever, weighing us down. We all need such places of ritual safekeeping. And I do believe that if your culture or tradition doesn't have the specific ritual you are craving, then you are absolutely permitted to make up a ceremony of your own devising, fixing your own broken-down emotional systems with all the do-it-yourself resourcefulness of a generous plumber/poet."

—ELIZABETH GILBERT

Death Over Donuts, an event where people can have a rare conversation about their mortality, was hosted in a synagogue in New York City on October 27th, 2018. The morning of the gathering, eleven members of the Tree of Life synagogue were shot and killed in Pittsburgh. Six were wounded.

Despite this tragedy, the organizers—Lab/Shul and Reboot—decided to still host the event. In fact, they even added a Shabbat service so that anyone in the area who was grieving could come to be in community and reflect.

I am not Jewish and only found out about the shooting when I was on the subway heading over. I was originally drawn to Death Over Donuts because I rarely get to discuss the end of life or have the space to think about what I want for my funeral. Yet, when I heard the news, I realized I would be an outsider coming into a sacred space of mourning. When I walked through the synagogue doors, I feared others would think I was intruding.

Yet if anything, the shooting brought an immediacy to my small group conversation that made us feel palpably connected. Unlike those people who were murdered at Tree of Life, we now had the opportunity to discuss how we would like to die. We could make plans. Through our discussion, we honored how lucky we were to be alive.

Once Death Over Donuts had ended, the facilitators gave everyone the opportunity to leave as they transitioned into the Sabbath portion of the evening. As chairs began to shift, I noticed that the room was filled with more people than before. New couples, families, and elderly folks—the widest range of ages I'd been around in a while—had joined us. These people were strangers to me, yet I could see the grief in their eyes. It felt almost too intimate to meet them in this way.

At this point, the names of the dead had not been released by the media. Everyone in that space was unsure if they had lost someone who was close to them. They just knew that the Jewish people had, yet again, been attacked.

With that feeling in the air, the rabbis encouraged everyone to move to the front of the room. "In moments like this, we should all be close to one another," Emily said. And with that, she began to sing a simple melody. Soon, the whole room had joined in, repeating the words over and over again.

When the song was done, the rabbis gave the room some space to talk about how they were feeling. People stood up to express fear that their family had died, anger their religion was being persecuted, and despair over the fact that the man who had killed so many people was also a loyal follower of Donald Trump. If they hadn't been given this space, those who stood up to share likely would have kept those thoughts inside. At the very least, they wouldn't have the supportive ears of tens of Jews, there to offer love and let them know their feelings were valid.

Afterward, a basket of mint was passed around for everyone to smell. This represented life, love, and renewal. It struck me how the simple gesture was so powerful in a moment where everyone was at a loss for what to do.

Finally, the group sang another song, arms wrapped around each other, and swayed in time to the music. Parents held their children and cried. Nieces and nephews hugged their grandparents. Husbands and wives held hands and closed their eyes tightly, as if they could shut out the painful thoughts that were entering their minds. Through it all, we sang.

And then, the music was over. The service was done. While the room still felt heavy, it also felt like something had been lifted. Within those walls was the power of a community demonstrating that it still had unity. There was a feeling of sacred sadness yet also sacred strength.

As Brené Brown beautifully says in *Braving the Wilderness*, "An experience of collective pain does not deliver us from grief or sadness; it is a ministry of presence. These moments remind us that we are not alone in our darkness and that our broken heart is connected to every heart that has known pain since the beginning of time."[31] Those Jewish traditions gave the community something to hold onto, and a sense of interconnection, even in the dark midst of mourning.

As I walked out of the synagogue toward the subway, a thought crossed my mind: "What would I do if someone close to me died?" And just as quickly, I realized that I had no idea. Other than my journaling and meditation practice, I have no prayers or traditions to fall back on. I suppose I would simply cry, call a friend, and feel helpless. And that doesn't feel like enough.

I have a deep yearning to be connected to sacredness in a way that only ancient traditions can offer. I'm sad that I don't have the faith to support that practice. Yet I also know I'm not the only one who feels this way. Hundreds of thousands of people in America have no religion and likely feel the same uncertainty around how to operate in times of tragedy.

Religion is there when we are at a loss for what to do. Yet without it, where do we turn?

THE THREE MOST POWERFUL RITUALS

As I was doing research for this book, I realized there's actually a scientific reason why I often feel like there aren't enough moments of deep connection in my life. It turns out, I'm frequently missing an essential part of the human experience—instances of "collective effervescence."

As Brené Brown explains in *Braving the Wilderness*, "Collective effervescence... is an experience of connection, communal emotion, and a 'sensation of sacredness' that happens when we are part of something that's bigger than us." People who frequently feel this way have a stronger sense of belonging in the world, which they achieve by engaging in moments of joy and pain with strangers. These experiences of collective assembly contribute to a life that is filled with a "sense of meaning, increased positive affect, an increased sense of social connection, and a decreased sense of loneliness."[31]

Researcher Shira Gabriel created the Tendency for Effervescent Assembly Measure, or TEAM scale, to measure how socially connected people feel. In her study, volunteers rated statements like: "Having giant blizzards or other events that close down a city or area are bad, but the feeling of connection to neighbors and even other strangers going through the same thing almost makes them worth it." People who regularly had experiences of collective assembly had a high TEAM score. They also were less lonely and had a greater sense of meaning and spiritual transcendence in their lives.[50]

This research shows that experiencing something en masse creates collective effervescence, which leads to a greater sense of well-being. Of course, while it's great to understand that, it's even better to know how we can intentionally create that experience within our own lives.[51]

It turns out, three of the most common rituals are used so often because they create feelings of collective effervesence quickly. But don't listen to me. Listen to science.

1) COLLECTIVE SONG

According to a 2015 study conducted by Eiluned Pearce, Jacques Launay, and Robin I.M. Dunbar, singing is the quickest way to get a group of people to feel connected. As the paper found, people who sing together, as opposed to people who don't sing together, feel closer more quickly. The researchers called it an "ice-breaker effect." Singing promoted faster group cohesion between strangers, which bypassed the need for people to get to know each other through conversation. The researchers concluded, "We argue that singing may have evolved to quickly bond large human groups of relative strangers, potentially through encouraging willingness to coordinate by enhancing positive affect."

In layman's terms, singing makes people feel happy and connected to each other.[52]

A different study showed that group singing is so powerful it literally increases people's ability to withstand pain. (I'm not sure who thought of testing this, but I love that they did!) The research, titled "Singing and social bonding: changes in connectivity and pain threshold as a function of group size," involved participants in a small choir of twenty to eighty people, and a mega choir of 232 people.

The results showed that feelings of inclusion, connectivity, positive affect, and measures of endorphin release all increased across singing rehearsals. They found that singing together, even within a large group where the participants don't know each other, fosters social closeness.[53]

These studies are a big reason why Robin Dunbar argues that singing is one of the best ways to make new friends. As he says in an interview for *Scientific American*, "Singing produces a massive hit of endorphins, and that makes you feel very bonded to the people with whom you're doing it."[54]

I experienced this exact phenomenon at a conference for pastors in New York City. (Sure, I'm not a pastor. But I was curious as hell about how people within that profession talk about community!) It was one of the first times I'd sung hymns in a group. Growing up, I would always half ass the songs in church. My logic was that I didn't want to be there, so I wouldn't sing the songs, either. Yet since I wasn't on my own turf at this conference, I decided to give it my all. To my surprise, I found myself being moved to tears by singing songs about Jesus with hundreds of other people. Even though I didn't believe the story behind the words, I felt tied to everyone in the room simply because we were singing together. In fact, at one point I even threw my hands up in the air and started swaying.

2) ACTS OF SYNCHRONICITY

Singing bonds groups because it's a synchronous activity—people do it together. As Dunbar has proven in his research, endorphin production is magnified when a group does the same thing at the same time.[55]

Can you think of a great way for a group to move with each other in sync? *Cough* Dance.

As a study called "Silent disco: dancing in synchrony leads to elevated pain thresholds and social closeness" explains, people participating in a synchronous dance have higher pain thresholds. That same group also felt more socially bonded. Out of all the movements tested in the study, the most effective at raising pain thresholds and social closeness was dance that was both synchronous and high energy.

Dunbar theorized in an interview with *The Washington Post* that a sense of belonging happens quickly with both song and dance because they can easily trigger trance states. "Once you've triggered that, you're in, I think, a different ballgame," he said. "(The sense of belonging) ramps up massively."

This science explains the flash mob craze of the early 2000s. All over the world, people started performing choreographed dances in public spaces. Some of my favorites include the Food Court Musical created by Improv Everywhere, the Bohemian Rhapsody flashmob, and twenty thousand people people dancing in time to the Black Eyed Peas "I Gotta Feeling" for Oprah's birthday.

Every time I watch a video of a flashmob, I cry my face off. And I'm not alone in that. One of the comments for a video called "Flashmob—The Sound of Silence" said:

"MADE ME CRY....And I'm a Combat Marine of five tours, didn't even cry at a funeral in my life, and I cried so hard seeing this. I have no idea why but it touched me like no other. THANK YOU GOOD PEOPLE WHO DID THIS, FROM A HARDCORE MARINE IN LAS VEGAS."[56]

I think flashmobs make so many people cry because they highlight the deep feelings of loneliness that so many people have but don't acknowledge. Watching hundreds of people collaborate to make something beautiful flies in the face of the internalized belief that we have to do everything ourselves, and that no one will ever help us. The reminder that we can support each other and make something beautiful together is enough to bring tears to anyone's eyes.

3) STORYTELLING

A study called "Storytelling as Adaptive Collective Sensemaking" says that the three main functions of storytelling are to enhance the reputation of the narrator, transmit important survival information, and maintain social bonds. Stories also clarify and strengthen intergroup identity.[57]

Of course, one of the most prevalent places for storytelling throughout history has been within religious services. Yet for those of us who don't attend, where can we go to feel connected to others and something that's larger than ourselves?

Medi Club, a monthly meditation and conversation group in New York City, is the perfect example of an event that utilizes storytelling to create group culture and strengthen bonds. Their original founders, Jesse Israel and Lauren Bille, would get up at every gathering to share what was happening in their lives. While they didn't name it, they were both courageously vulnerable because they wanted everyone else in the room to do the same with each other.

I'll never forget one gathering where the two talked about the fight they were having as leaders and roommates. They shared that they were struggling, and even attending friendship counseling to make it work. Yet in the end, Lauren decided to leave Medi Club and pursue her own projects. Yet she didn't decide and then transition out quietly. She was fearless enough to stand in front of the room, alongside Jesse, and tell the community about the changes that were about to happen.

Jesse and Lauren's bravery spoke to the group identity that they were striving to create. By telling that story, they were saying, "The people in this room work on our shit. We're not afraid to talk about the hard stuff." By being vulnerable enough to share, they also enhanced their own reputation. If that was someone's first time at Medi Club, they would have immediately trusted its leaders. After all, they had just exposed their own weaknesses to a room of 150 people.

After the two shared, everyone got into groups of four to discuss a prompt: "What's an area of your life where you want to make a big change? What would happen if you did it?" If this question was posed to the room without the storytelling, people would undoubtedly feel uncomfortable and like too much was being asked of them. Yet following

Jesse and Lauren's story, the discussion made total sense. Suddenly, a room of people who didn't know each other were leaning in to hear stories from their neighbors about divorces, career changes, and reunions with estranged parents. This sharing with strangers, as I've mentioned before, is a key way for people to feel like they're less alone. Mix that with the braveness of vulnerability, and you've got a room that's buzzing with people who are excited to reconnect and keep the conversation going. That wouldn't be possible without leaders who have the courage to share their truth, even when it's not pretty.

COMBINING THE RITUALS

It's 10:45 a.m. on a Saturday. Friends and strangers slowly trickle into a cozy space in Melbourne, Australia. They're immediately welcomed at the door by two friendly volunteers as well as a big table of coffee and snacks. Light music plays in the background while anyone who's new is introduced to a regular.

From hearing this description, you might assume this room has some crosses and a few Jesuses scattered around. Yet this isn't a religious gathering. Instead, it's The Weekly Service—a secular gathering where people share stories, listen to music, pause for reflection and engage in conversation. The gathering has been a prominent part of the Melbourne community since September 2015... and it all started because of grilled meat.

Back in late 2014, Cam Elliot and Chris Churchill were hanging out at a barbecue. After a few burgers, the conversation eventually turned to religion. That's when the two friends realized they'd both had a similar epiphany. They didn't align with any mainstream faith, but they loved the idea of church. Both of them were inspired by the rituals, the music, the community, and the space to think about important ideas like gratitude and grace. Yet at the same time, neither of them felt comfortable in a church service.

So, they decided to make their own... minus the religion.

After years of trial and error, The Weekly Service has turned into a well-oiled machine. The organizers have created a consistent format that provides a sense of stability—yet enough surprises to keep people engaged and coming back.

The theme of a recent gathering was grief. Cam was nervous that the topic would be too heavy and attendees would not be comfortable enough to share. Regardless, he took a risk and stuck with it.

As with every Weekly Service, the group started with a grounding meditation. As Cam told me, "It's easier for people to be present when their minds are clear."

Once the meditation had ended, Cam stood to ask everyone a question. "Today's theme is grief," he said. "So what I'd like to know is, why are you here? Take a moment to think about it, and then share with a partner."

The room was quiet for a moment and then slowly started to buzz with discussion.

After a few minutes, Cam raised his hand to get everyone's attention. "Alright!" he called out over the conversation. "Does anyone want to share with the room why they chose to be here today?"

Some of the answers included:

"I spend a lot of time rushing around. This is the place where I come to stop. I don't have anywhere else like that."

"I don't make space for grief in my life. And I know I need to."

"There's something not right about the way I'm living my life—and the way I see my friends living. I want to reimagine my future, and I want to do it with other people."

"I need to change the types of conversations I'm having."

Those words hung in the air and gave a sense of meaning to the space. With those few shares, everyone in the room knew they were part of something that was different than their daily lives. They were in an alternate universe—a co-created reality that was different than the one they left on the street.

With that, the week's speaker stood up and shared her story. She was nervous, and for good reason. She bravely shared about how her parents had recently died, and how she never reached the level of depth in their relationship that she wanted. She wasn't just mourning the passing of her parents. She was grieving the fact that she'd never have the chance to improve her relationship with them.

When she finished her story, the room was quiet. It was impossible to tell how her words had landed. Did people love the story? Were they upset? Cam didn't know, and it was clear that the storyteller was feeling exposed after sharing such a vulnerable story. So, Cam decided to share his appreciation for the storyteller's bravery. "I so appreciate you," he said. "Because of your vulnerability, I see you. Thank you for that."

After that, an audience member raised their hand. And then another. Soon, the entire room was thanking her for sharing. "I could see her opening up," Cam said. "Soon she was glowing."

Once the rounds of appreciation were done, people started sharing their own experiences of loss. "I relate to this phenomenon of a 'high dream,'" someone said. "I had all these lofty ambitions to repair a relationship and make it amazing. But then that person died, so I never got the chance."

Another man shared his regrets around never making an effort to get closer to his father. "I've never said this to anyone," he admitted. It was his first Weekly Service.

The fact that a complete newcomer to this space could share something so bravely is no accident. Cam and his team have worked for years to create a space where people are confident that they will be taken care of. "People share because they have a sense of trust in the thing we created," Cam said. "But more importantly, they have a sense of trust with each other."

This feeling of belonging has been building, piece by piece, for years. Now the organization is at a place where people are comfortable with some experimentation. "We're at a point where the container can hold more risk," Cam said.

For example, at one service a storyteller backed out at the last minute. Cam had to stand at the front of the room, look at everyone who committed their time to being there, and say, "We don't have a story for today. So we need to figure this out together."

The group decided to use a polling app to measure the themes that people had the most interest in speaking about. After a few minutes, the winners were "fun," "silly," "play," and "trust." Then, without Cam even needing to prompt them, four storytellers came up to share their experiences with those words. The evening ended with the entire room making up a song together.

"It won't be winning any Grammys any time soon," Cam laughed. "But it's ours."

INCORPORATING RITUAL INTO YOUR DAILY LIFE

If you don't live in Australia, you unfortunately can't attend The Weekly Service. And if you're in a smaller town, there probably aren't a ton of flash mobs popping up. So how can you experience some of these rituals on a more regular basis?

Singing: If you really want to master the art of singing, a local choir is always an option. But that's probably too much of a commitment if you simply want to belt out a few tunes. Some other options include karaoke, piano bars, and singing at a concert. Another thing to Google in your area is "circle singing," where people gather in a circle for an improvised singing session. If you're feeling shy, or simply don't live in an area with a ton of options, you can always screen your favorite musical and invite some friends over to scream-sing along.

Dancing: I'm a huge fan of a few global dance communities. One is Ecstatic Dance, which encourages all movement styles. No experience is needed. You can stretch, do cartwheels, or just bop along to the DJ. Every city has a different scene. You can attend almost every day of the week in San Francisco and Oakland, where partner dancing is really popular. In New York City you can check it out roughly every other week. Hundreds of people attend the event on both coasts. Talking and cell phones are not allowed on the dance floor, and the space is sober.

If you want something a little more facilitated, or there simply isn't an Ecstatic Dance in your area, try 5Rhythms. This movement practice uses five different tempos of movement—Flowing, Staccato, Chaos, Lyrical and Stillness. When followed in sequence, they're called a "wave." Each 5Rhythms typically lasts two hours, which equals two waves. Again, no dance experience is needed. In New York, all ages and ability levels are welcome. You'll just as likely see a five-year-old as someone who's eighty or in a wheelchair. It's truly inclusive and one of the most diverse dance spaces I've been to. Simply look up either "Ecstatic Dance" or "5Rhythms" plus your state or country on Google, and I'm sure you'll find something.

Storytelling: Storytelling shows are popular all over the world. Simply attending one, and hearing the stories of strangers, is a great way to feel connected to the people in your town. The Moth is the most well-known, and has shows all over the world. There's even performances that allow people to tell their story onstage for the first time. In New York, storytelling is so popular that there's a Facebook group—aptly named "NYC Storytelling"—with almost six thousand members. Yet even if you don't live in a big city, you should be able to find an open mic night.

Can't find anywhere to share your story or hear others? Start your own show! There's no better way to feel connected to your community and make new friends than to start your own gathering. If that's the route you choose to take, remember: consistency is key. Choose the same day every month, like the third Wednesday, and stick to it. You'll have regulars in no time!

KEY TAKEAWAYS

- Experiences of collective effervescence are directly tied to a happy and healthy life.

- The three most powerful rituals are collective song, acts of synchronicity, and storytelling.
- Religion is extremely useful in times of tragedy. Without it, we need other rituals to get us through difficult times.

QUESTIONS TO CONSIDER

- How can we create more public rituals that incorporate song, dance, and storytelling?
- Where can we hold consistent rituals for the public, other than religious buildings?
- What spaces allow for communal grieving outside of religion? How can we create more of them?

8

STEPPING INTO LEADERSHIP

"You cannot change any society unless you take responsibility for it, unless you see yourself as belonging to it and responsible for changing it."

—GRACE LEE BOGGS

I knew I wanted to be a freelance writer when I moved to New York. Yet there was a slight problem with that plan... I'd never met someone who was a self-employed wordsmith before. Since I didn't have that community, it was difficult to believe that career was possible for me. So, taking the same approach that I did with my social life, I started going to networking events by myself.

Slowly, I started to find other solopreneur writers. I met with a few in a coffee shop to complain about our editors. I gathered with a group at the New York Public Library to swap contacts for magazine publications. Yet, despite all the people I was meeting, I didn't feel like I was improving my skill set. Despite some pretty thorough Googling, I couldn't find any courses to teach me how to use writing as a financially sustainable career option. Granted, this was six years ago. Those sorts of courses are far more popular now. Yet at the time, my resources were truly limited.

After plenty of mistakes and a few strokes of good luck, I'd figured out how to make it as a writer in New York City. By that point, I had people asking me for advice constantly. They all wanted to know how to be self-employed without living on Ramen and peanut butter alone.

I kept looking around the city, trying to find some sort of class that would teach freelancers how to thrive. Yet I couldn't. So, even though I had no idea what I was doing, I decided to create a conference with my friend, Melissa Wong. Hustle Fest was a full-day conference to teach aspiring solopreneurs how to go "full-time to freelance." It was exactly what we both wished we had when we started our careers.

The original Hustle Fest was in the basement of Melissa's community center, New Women Space. It was a hot day in

July, and over one hundred people were packed into the tiny room. Halfway through the day, the air conditioner broke. I was sure everyone would leave, but they were so desperate for the information that they stuck around. Sure, they were covered in sweat, but they got the tools they'd been craving. Despite the bazillion degree temperature, we still got glowing reviews from our guests.

I created Hustle Fest because I couldn't find the space I desperately wanted, and I knew that if I wanted it, other people did, too. So I created it with Melissa, even though we were both scared and there was a voice in our heads that said, "Who are you to do this?" At twenty-three years old, I was even more scared than Melissa. I legitimately had a fear that someone would yell out, "Who the hell are you? You're a baby? You can't tell us anything!"

Yet in reality, even though I was young, people were simply grateful that I had the courage to build the space they were desperate for. That's how people will feel when you bring them together. I promise. Even if there aren't enough chairs, or only two people show up, or the food is burned, they will be grateful that you cared enough to invite them in the first place. Trust me on this one.

The world needs more people who are bold enough to call themselves gatherers. These wizards of connection create an opportunity to reduce the suffering of people who feel isolated. Gatherers are the leaders who make the world less lonely. As David T. Hsu says in his study on isolation, "Untethered," solving Americans' increasing sense of isolation requires "advocates for the most isolated among us; passionate community-builders from every sector; entrepreneurs obsessed with building new and refurbished solutions for this age-old problem; visionary funders to advance the agenda; artists and storytellers with a gift for continually revealing our condition."[8]

So, my friend, consider this book your permission slip. It's written with your favorite pen, and it's on some really fancy paper. After you open the envelope—getting the slightest hint of that scent you love—you read this:

"You, the person whose hands are touching this page, have full permission to call yourself a gatherer. You have felt that achy gap in your life—the place where you wish community existed—and have the confidence to alchemize that pain into a space that soothes the same wound for many others.

"You understand this will be difficult and know you will make mistakes. Yet you also understand that the act of gathering is healing for everyone involved. You are confident in your knowledge that your community needs more connection and trust that you have the heart to make it happen."

If you're scared just thinking about this, awesome. That means you care. The world needs more people like that.

HOW TO STEP UP

I'm hoping that at this point, you feel compelled to bring people together. Some sort of gathering is missing in your life, and you want to make it happen. I've been at this point before, and I know how exciting it feels. Yet it's easy to get overwhelmed if you don't consider some important factors. Before you throw up that Eventbrite and start inviting all your friends, consider these questions:

How many resources do I have? Bringing people together can take a lot of time, money, and energy. That's why you should think about how much bandwidth you actually have before you commit to taking a project on. Events are the most enjoyable and sustainable when the organizer feels recharged by it rather than drained.

Who can help me? With that in mind, any project is made easier—and more fun!—with help. What elements of this gathering will you not enjoy putting together, but someone you know might? For example, finding a venue for my events is a huge pain. Thankfully, my friend Tony runs a consultancy that helps people grow their coworking space. They're always looking for new ways to bring people through their doors.

Offering The Joy List Social at their office is a win for them, and for me!

Pro tip: I can get these spaces for free if I email my guests a code for a free day of coworking the following week. This works especially well if a group of people from my event show up together. It helps people deepen their relationship, and brings new business to the coworking space.

How can I test this quickly and cheaply? If you're anything like me, you want to throw a big event right off the bat. But please, learn from my mistakes and look before you leap. It's wise to do a MVG, or minimum viable gathering, before you throw a big blowout. Do something with a small group who's willing to give you honest feedback, and go from there.

Who is this really for? While this sounds obvious, it's crucial to nail down who the audience for your event is. This understanding will influence everything from the way you describe your gathering on Facebook to where you promote it. Even if you want to throw a dinner party for your friends, get more specific! Is this only for the friends you're really close with and want to prioritize spending quality time with? Is this for people who you don't know really well and want to understand their inner world? Taking a little bit of time to consider who's invited will make a big difference.

ACKNOWLEDGE WHO'S PRESENT

I want the guests at my events to feel at home. Yet as a woman who comes from an abundance of privilege—being white, heterosexual, able-bodied, upper-class, and college educated—I can unintentionally create spaces that are not welcoming to people who are different from me.

Throughout my experience running events—creating a conference for freelancers, facilitating conversation circles for business owners, organizing a camp for people who are interested in social justice—I have hurt people with my ignorance.

For example, I have hosted events in spaces that were not wheelchair or handicap accessible. It did not even cross my mind to warn attendees of that fact in advance. I have organized an all-white panel, only to realize once the event started what a mistake I'd made. I have also been a participant in all-white panels and struggled with the discomfort of saying something to the event organizer.

To be honest, there have been times when I haven't spoken up. Yet through these experiences, I have learned that my own momentary discomfort means that someone else can walk into a space and feel like they are welcome.

I am constantly learning and re-learning how to dive into uncomfortable conversations, own my mistakes, and offer a genuine apology. It has been a humbling process to discover that, while it was not my intention to hurt someone through my gathering, I can still make a negative impact. In fact, sometimes my presence as a white person alone is damaging.

Beverly Daniel Tatum, a psychologist and professor at Spelman College who focuses on race relations, frequently uses this exercise in her classroom: "Complete the sentence 'I am___' with as many descriptors as you can think of in sixty seconds."

After years of reading students' answers, she's noticed a trend. Students of color typically mention their racial or ethnic group while white students rarely do the same.

As Tatum explains in her book, *Why Are All the Black Kids Sitting Together in the Cafeteria?,* women also usually mention being female while men often don't mention their maleness. Jewish students will say they are Jews while mainline Protestants don't mention their religion. A student who is gay, lesbian, or bisexual will mention their sexuality while those who are straight will rarely think to list that aspect of themselves.

Why does this happen? Tatum summarizes the psychology behind the pattern far more eloquently than I could:

"Common across these examples is that in the areas where a person is a member of the dominant or advantaged social group, the category is usually not mentioned. That element of their identity is so taken for granted by them that it goes without comment. It is taken for granted by them because it is taken for granted by the dominant culture."

As a member of many dominant cultures, it is easy for me to avoid the question of "Who is this event for?" Yet as I've started creating more spaces, I've challenged myself to look at my audience more closely and consciously try to make it more welcoming to a variety of different people.[58]

The next time you're bringing people together, I challenge you to really look at who shows up. Are you hosting a meditation that's mostly for upper-class white folks? Does your tech meetup have seventy-five percent men? Acknowledging this is an important first step. Then, it's up to you. Do you double down on who you're catering to or start actively working to diversify who shows up? If you do neither, any attendee who does not fall within your norms will likely feel uncomfortable. They will also feel less connected to the group because the audience for the gathering is unclear.

For example, I've had folks over the age of forty ask me if my events are diverse in their age range. This question brought a harsh reality to light. Most people who show up in my spaces are between the ages of twenty-two and thirty-five. Yet at the same time, the intention of my series, The Joy List Social, is to give *anyone* the opportunity to show up alone and leave with new friends.

"To be honest, I'm not comfortable with that," one woman who is in her fifties told me. "I don't want to be the only old lady in the crowd."

For future events, I'm planning on explicitly labeling them as intergenerational, and encouraging folks to bring their children *and* older friends. If I never name this intention, things will always stay the same—yet another event for young people rather than a rare space where people of any age group can feel welcome.

LESSONS FROM THE FIELD

After attending many events that have done a great job of creating an inclusive atmosphere—as well as some that haven't—I've learned a few key lessons.

Lead with listening: I'm the type of person who loves to say, "I'll do it!" I happily step into the spotlight to speak in front of a crowd or organize a group of people. Yet oftentimes, the best person to speak isn't the first one who volunteers. As an Asian American friend of mine said at a dinner party, "Americans are socialized to have their voices heard. Yet in Asia, a sign of maturity is to think of your community first." Because of that upbringing, she can struggle to get a word in edgewise in group conversations.

As a facilitator, it's important to keep an eye on who is speaking, as well as who has not uttered a word. There will always be people who dominate the conversation. As the host, it is your job to stop those people—even if it means interrupting them—in order to give others the chance to speak. A line I like to use is, "I'm so sorry to cut you off. Before you continue, I want to make sure I give everyone the chance to speak. I noticed that this side of the table hasn't contributed. What do you think?" Sometimes people need to be explicitly called on in order to share, and then they will enthusiastically jump into the conversation.

Get comfortable with discomfort: As a community builder, it's your responsibility to name who your space is for—and who it's not for. As Priya Parker says in *The Art of Gathering*, "Gatherings that please everyone occur, but they rarely thrill. Gatherings that are willing to be alienating—which is different from *being* alienating—have a better chance to dazzle... The more focused and particular a gathering is, the more narrowly it frames itself and the more passion it arouses."[59]

For example, I'm the cofounder of a meetup called NYC Community Builders. Every month, we bring gatherers together to learn new skills, discuss the issues within our own community, and ask for help. One meeting, ironically around how to have difficult conversations, we stumbled into an issue with our attendees. We were pretty loose with who could attend, figuring that anyone who showed up at an event marked "community builders" would be organizing one of their own. Yet we were wrong. At one point, a man started monopolizing the conversation with a story about a personal issue with his friend. While the moderators eventually managed to get the conversation back on track, we still wasted a lot of everyone's time. (This also highlights the importance of deciding your "bad cop" timekeeper before the event.)

After that evening, we made a new rule: "You must be able to contribute to the conversation. Only people who currently run a community, or are actively planning a new one, are welcome at these events."

Step outside yourself: When I started The Joy List, I only listed the events I had attended myself. Yet after a few months, I had an embarrassing realization. This newsletter is intended to reduce loneliness for *everyone*, but I'm only featuring the communities that are helpful for *me*. That's when I started asking for other people to send events that I likely wouldn't hear about, yet are great places for people to make friends. Now The Joy List features conversation circles for black fathers, open mics for the queer community, and yoga for people of color.

Even though I started The Joy List with the best of intentions, I failed to realize that everything I chose was filtered through my own personal lens. If I truly wanted to help a broader audience in New York find community, I knew I needed to publicly ask for help and source events that I would likely never hear of or be able to attend myself.

THE ELEPHANT IN THE ROOM

I have a confession.

Up until this point, I've been withholding something from you. And I know that once I acknowledge it, the honeymoon phase in your relationship with community building might end. Suddenly you'll find yourself noticing some wrinkles, hating its laugh, and wondering how you ignored that it never, ever takes out the trash. In other words, you'll realize that the art of gathering is not as perfectly sexy as you once thought.

Yet, I want this relationship to last. And that means acknowledging the shadow side of community building. It's not easy to look at, yet essential to acknowledge if you want a deep understanding of gathering. So, here we go.

The American system is not set up to reward gatherers—emotionally or financially.

If you choose to embark on the path of community building, I'm here to let you know that it's going to be a struggle. There is no ladder to climb. There is no how-to manual to follow. It's just you, making it up as you go. While I wish there was an abundance of resources to support you, there simply aren't. Part of the responsibility of being a gatherer is creating the tools for future generations, like how-to guides and videos. Because right now? They're pretty few and far between.

I know this because I've looked for guidance in community building everywhere from Harvard Divinity School and church planting conferences to political organizing. Yet while these resources are helpful, they're not exactly what I want—help for someone who wants to create something that's as deeply impactful as a religious experience, minus the whole God part.

Over the years, I've had many conversations with friends where we dream about the ideal program to support us in our community building. In it, leaders would teach us how to develop our group, set personal boundaries, find aligned brand partnerships, and earn enough money to thrive. Sometimes, it feels like being a modern gatherer has all the struggles of entrepreneurship without the prestige.

There were times when writing this book that I wanted to slam my laptop shut and yell, "What? Is everyone who brings people together supposed to be a martyr, sacrificing themselves emotionally, financially, and physically for the sake of community? How do we recharge? How can we take care of ourselves?"

The phenomenon of "organizer burnout" is referenced regularly in the progressive social justice space. In fact, it's so common that there's even a way to measure it—the Maslach Burnout Inventory. According to mindgarden, the research institute behind the study, burnout is defined as "A syndrome of emotional exhaustion, depersonalization, and reduced personal accomplishment that can occur among individuals who work with people in some capacity." Sound familiar?

The reasons behind burnout in the inventory are:

- Workload (too much work, not enough resources)
- Control (micromanagement, lack of influence, accountability without power)

- Reward (not enough pay, appreciation, or satisfaction)
- Community (isolation, conflict, disrespect)
- Fairness (discrimination, favoritism)
- Values (ethical conflicts, meaningless tasks)

Once you've discovered which areas you're suffering in, it's easier to create a game plan to create some positive change.[60] Anyone whose work centers around caring for others can struggle with giving love back to themselves. Thankfully, you can take some small steps to make sure you stay stable.

THE UNSAID BASICS OF SELF-CARE

I've learned a handful of important lessons after being in the gathering space for a few years. While all of them seem obvious, they're easily forgotten in the daily rush of to-do lists and endless appointments. Just writing them down was an important reminder to myself that these things matter. So, for your benefit and my own, here are some key learnings to keep in mind as you venture into the world of community building.

Talk to other organizers regularly: Leading a community can be lonely. Personally, it feels like I'm supposed to be the bright light of the room, maintaining a smile and a positive attitude no matter what. Yet keeping this attitude, while also having no one to discuss the difficulties that I'm going through with, is a recipe for flaming out and resenting my community.

A lack of support is a big reason why I started a monthly gathering for community builders in New York City. I wanted a space to admit that I was struggling and reach out for help.

Despite my big dreams, the start of our first meeting was a disaster. The only subway line to our location was shut down, meaning it would take some people three times as long to get to the space. As a result, only a handful of people were there right on time—while thirty were an hour late. One of them was my co-organizer, who had the run of show and the snacks. My anxiety levels immediately went through the roof.

I asked Peter Block, the author of *Community*, via email about the moments when he feels the loneliest as an organizer. To be honest, I wasn't expecting a reply. He's a busy man. So when I got an answer, I was delighted and then immediately perplexed by what I read: "On the question of being out of place, there is a loneliness to this work that never goes away and a feeling that there is something wrong with us for the way we see the world. Both of these are true. I can find a place where I belong and still at times, or even most of the time, feel completely out of place. That's what it means to be a human being."

Even though his point is a little sad, it totally resonated with me. I'm the founder of The Joy List, and the host of The Joy List Social. If anyone should feel comfortable in that space, it should be me. Yet I'm still finding my footing as an organizer. Since a million things are going through my mind at every event, it's hard to feel present in conversations and enjoy the gathering. It's not for me. It's for other people. As a result, I can ironically feel alone in the space I created. Most of the attendees haven't hosted a large event before, so they don't understand why I seem a little scattered. Yet in reality, putting on an event requires a lot of energy. Once it comes to showtime, I have limited resources to give to my guests. Ironically, the result is that I feel like an outsider at the event I created to reduce loneliness. I'm still trying to figure out how to feel more at home and conserve my energy before the event begins.

Set boundaries: This is a key tip for anyone who wants to make community-building their full-time job. I understand that when you're so deeply passionate about your work, it becomes a vocation. As a result, it's easy for it to fill every waking minute of your life. Yet that's a recipe for burnout. One tip I give everyone in my Facebook group, NYC Community Builders, is to time box your day. I like to start my day with an hour of journaling, reading, and meditating. Then I get some work done before a 10 to 11 a.m. yoga class. Between noon and 6:30 p.m. is work time. After 7:30 p.m., I always make sure I have something scheduled. This could be a date, or an event, or dinner with a friend. Yet I know myself, and if something isn't in my calendar, I will keep working!

Casper ter Kuile, one of the founders of How We Gather, enforces a tech sabbath for himself every week. This means that between Friday and Saturday, he doesn't use email or social media at all. As he says on his website, "In an effort to make more time for reading fiction, to have a break from feeling held ransom by my inbox, and as an exercise in humility, I've been turning off my laptop and phone for twenty-four hours every Friday night at dusk. I have created a little ritual—lighting a candle, singing a song—and enter 'tech sabbath' time. It's like taking a vacation every week—truly."

Have accountability: Accountability isn't just useful for going to the gym or writing your novel. It's also a great tool for remembering to take care of yourself. For example, I use Focusmate, a website that pairs you with a virtual coworking buddy, every morning at 7:30 a.m. This time is for my morning routine. Without someone waiting for me on my computer, it's easy for me to skip making time for myself. Yet with Focusmate, I know that someone else will be impacted if I don't show up.

Another great way to ensure that you take a break is to plan a vacation with other community builders. They understand, more than many other people, how hard it can be to step away from your projects. Enforce a "no work talk" rule, leave your computer at home, and turn your phone on airplane mode. Even one unplugged weekend away can make a world of difference and will deepen your relationships far more quickly than if you were staring at your screens.

Surround yourself with people whose lives are an inspiration: As motivational speaker Jim Rohn once said, we are the average of the five people we spend the most time with.[61] So look around. Do the people in your life take care of themselves? Do they inspire you to take care of your beautiful body, have conversations that leave you glowing, and make you feel positively wonderful in their presence? If not, it might be time to re-prioritize who you spend time with.

Sure, you might have family obligations, colleagues you need to deal with, and board members who need to be chatted up. Yet outside of that small circle, you get to choose your community. And if you are intentional with who you surround yourself with, rather than going with the default of age-old friends and folks from work, magic can happen. For example, today I'm going to an intimate gathering with a revered Buddhist teacher because my friend who's in a ten-year teacher training program invited me. Yesterday, a physical therapist pal told me the story of how he helped a woman with cancer dance again. And this week alone I've been invited to a dinner for intentional community builders, a sober dance party, a 1500-person meditation, and a masquerade birthday party on a yacht. All of those organizers are my friends.

I'm not saying this to brag. (Although, after years of surrounding myself with people who I felt like crap around, I'm pretty darn proud of myself.) This is a reminder that there are freakin' extraordinary people out there, and they need friends, too. You just have to find them—and they're probably not at the same bar you've been going to every Friday night for five years.

Tap into pleasure: America's pervasive workaholism is a symptom of a society where we are taught that being productive is good and relaxation is bad. We exercise to get results rather than to feel joy in our bodies. We eat for fuel instead of enjoyment. We brag about "hustling" and "grinding" because a lack of time is a status symbol rather than a sign that we should slow down and take a break.

LiYana Silver, author of *Feminine Genius*, argues in her book that we are living in a time that is dominated by the Divine Masculine.[62] Everything with a feminine essence, from listening to our bodies to finding pleasure in our sexuality, is often left in the corner. "I can come back to those things once I've finished everything on my to-do list," we tell ourselves. "I only deserve to feel good once the work is done." Yet let's be real. The list is always growing. Taking time to slow down now is a gift to our future selves. By stopping for a break, even when there is more to do, we send ourselves love and remember that we are more than our accomplishments. We deserve a long walk and a bath even if that big presentation isn't finished yet!

FILLING THE CUP

A few years ago, Katie Gordon was at a gathering for spiritual innovators and community builders. Amidst a mostly young crowd of organizers, Katie went to talk to two Catholic Sisters who were there as elders. She asked, "What are your reflections after being surrounded by all of these energized community leaders?"

Their answer shocked Katie and has stuck with her ever since:

"We're worried about you. You create community for others, yet you're all also expecting to receive community in return as you build it. You're going to wear yourselves out doing so."

Remembering that moment, Katie laughed. "I thought they were going to be glowing, so inspired by all of these young people who are fighting to create change," she said. "And instead, they gave me that."

The life of a Catholic Sister, compared to one of a modern-day event organizer, is vastly different. Yet their purpose is similar. Both want to help others feel like they are "seen." They want everyone who walks through their doors to know they are welcome, they matter, and their voice will be heard. Sisters and event organizers want the people they interact with to feel like part of something that's bigger than themselves. They want people to feel uplifted by the presence of a different energy, whether that's God or the power of a group of people coming together.

However, there are huge differences between Sisters and gatherers that makes a crucial difference in their quality of life—the integration of ritual.

"Women religious are a part of long-standing traditions in religious life," Katie said. "It provides the structure for them to both receive from and contribute to community."

Monastic communities, for instance, take a vow of stability, which means they are committed to staying rooted in one place. "As a result, their relationships are all rooted in that place, and by staying there, they're able to understand that community and its needs so deeply," Katie said.

Telling other young people about the vow of stability, a generation that is largely thought of as transient and digital nomads, she thought they wouldn't understand the vow of stability. But actually, they loved it. Katie said, "We're so hungry for that type of stability, for a commitment to place and to people, but I don't think we even realize it."

Meanwhile, event creators who are not religiously affiliated are trying to do the sacred work of gathering... without the strong foundation of community to help sustain them. As Katie explained, "Sometimes I'm so busy creating spaces of community for others that I'm not even receiving nourishment from it myself. And that's a problem."

OVERCOMING BURNOUT

Cam loves running The Weekly Service, a curated secular gathering on Saturday mornings where people share stories, listen to music, pause for reflection and engage in conversation. It's an important part of his life, and he's put enormous amounts of energy, money, and time into making the project into a reality. Having connected, emotional conversations with his attendees filled him up and made him feel useful. Yet one week he surprised himself by thinking: "If anyone else asks me for help, I'm going to lose it. I can't take it anymore."

This moment is a point that a lot of gatherers, including myself, can recognize—organizer burnout.

Suddenly, Cam didn't get energized when one of his regulars asked for his help with a personal problem. Instead, he felt resentful. "I was tired all the time," Cam told me. "I was questioning the purpose of the thing I created. This thought just kept going around in my head: 'Are we just a bunch of middle class white people getting together to feel good about ourselves? Is that enough?'"

Part of this questioning resulted in some great changes for the organization, including an initiative to make the space more diverse. Yet it also highlighted some weaknesses in the organization. Cam didn't feel like he was getting enough support and was suffering emotionally as a result.

I asked Cam to explain why he felt so burned out. His response was so wonderfully put that I've included it in full:

"I'd taken on a caretaker role with The Weekly Service. That's traditionally a woman's job. I had never been trained in the art of hosting: looking after people, holding space for them, making sure they have what they need. Suddenly, I was like a counselor for eighty people, both at the event and outside of it. It was extremely time intensive, for very low pay. And while all of that was going on, I was also dealing with the stresses

of making the project financially sustainable. It was draining me. Not being valued by people hurts.

"But to be honest, as long as we have the patriarchy, this work won't be seen as important. People don't value caretaking. And that sucks because we're not just putting on events. We're doing deep work. We're soul workers."

My next question to Cam was obvious: "So, how do you deal with the burnout?"

To be honest, I was hoping his answer would be simple. Drink more water. Eat more protein. Do some yoga in the morning. Unfortunately, the response was a little more complex.

"The work we do is deeply personal," he said. "We care so much, but we can't be attached to the outcome. For example, I think I can control the outcome of an event. But I can't. That's an illusion. All I can do is be of service in the moment."

As he spoke, I'll admit that I thought, "Great. This sounds like managing my energy is going to be even *more* work." And I was right.

When I told Cam that I feel a huge energy drain the day after my events, he explained that I was experiencing an adrenaline hangover. I was "operating from my adrenals," meaning that I was stretching myself thin and caring about too many things at once. I was thinking about who was taking out the trash while also attempting to engage in a deep and meaningful conversation. On a broader scale, my problem was that I was obsessing about an extrinsic goal—hosting a flawless event—rather than an intrinsic goal—creating the conditions for people to form new friendships. "You weren't operating from a pure place," Cam told me. "You need to reframe from an obsessive passion, which is all about things you can't control, to a harmonious passion, which comes from joy."

The hardest part for me to wrap my head around was that an obsessive passion is tied into ego: wanting people to like me because of my event and thinking of it as an external representation of my worth. I wanted people to think I'm smart and see me as a leader. Of course, I can't really control any of those things. It's not healthy for me to hold on to those outcomes.

Cam's biggest lesson to me was this: "Don't let your ego get in the way of your presence. That's what drains you."

I'm starting to work on it, yet I also know I need to be patient with myself. I've been conditioned to be achievement-oriented for my entire life. It's going to take some serious work to unlearn those habits.

LEARNING TO RECEIVE

Leading a community is not the same as having one yourself.

Gatherers need friendship outside of the spaces they're building. These relationships, the ones that are outside of the stressors of your "work" life, can be immensely recharging. Personally, it is essential for me to have people in my life who cared about me before I started The Joy List. Their world does not revolve around bringing other people together. In fact, they'd rather talk about anything else. As someone who is constantly in conversation about community, this is hugely refreshing. These relationships are the breath of fresh air I need to dive into my work with new life.

Being a community builder, it's easy for me to constantly create the spaces I wish to see in the world. Yet there's a big problem with that. I'm always the one in charge and never get to participate.

Think about the people you know you are constant givers. (Hint: you might be one.) The teacher who pays for supplies with her own paycheck yet won't the spend any money on something for herself. The yoga teacher who is constantly guiding others yet never has time for their own practice. Or the nonprofit worker who is checking their email so frequently they can't even sit through a movie without leaving the theater. These people are all around us and represent a much larger problem. Taking care of ourselves is seen as a luxury, rather than a necessity.

As Parker Palmer says in *The Courage to Teach*, "When I violate myself, I invariably end up violating the people I work with."[63] When our batteries are not charged, we cannot give fully to others. That is why gatherers need a rich community life outside of the one they have built, where they can receive love and care without worry of immediately needing to return it. Relationships in community are all about long game. You don't need to worry about returning the love right now because you know you'll be together for years. Those types of relationships are invaluable and should be deeply treasured. How many teachers inflict their own pain on their students, the pain that comes from doing what never was, or no longer is, their true work.

In good faith, I can't ask you to become a gatherer without admitting that our society doesn't value it. As Cam mentioned, caring for others is traditionally women's work, which means that it's not seen as having prestige or monetary value. However, there are a variety of ways to bring people together, large and small, that all have the power to create connection.

To give you some inspiration for creating the future of community building, consider these questions that Casper and Angie propose in "Care of Souls":

Who will step up and create:

- *A loneliness tax on Netflix and Amazon that goes to supporting Gatherers?*
- *A Care of Souls career path that leads from high school through major university programs in Healing, Making, and Venturing?*
- *An ICO for a Stewarding macrostructure for the Care of Souls field, which includes health insurance?*
- *A Spiritual Innovation Lab that incubates and finances the work of Makers and Gatherers in creating new community rituals?*
- *An online matching platform for Novices to connect with Masters in their roles?*
- *A Venturer-backed line of credit to replace the two-year grant cycle for new efforts in this field?*
- *A media outlet dedicated to disseminating the wisdom of Elders and Seers?*

As their team notes in the report, "Resistance is insufficient without a better alternative."[40] Together, we will find the solutions and start creating a world where the healing act of gathering is highly valued.

For now, everyone can make smaller changes to bring more healthy congregation into their everyday life. Use an icebreaker to deepen the conversation of your nightly family dinners. Have a discussion after movie night with your friends. Invite your colleagues to take a deep breath together before the big meeting. These tiny changes can feel vulnerable because they show that you want to feel closer to others. That's vulnerable, but as if I've said before, anything that's scary is worth doing. Your community will thank you.

KEY TAKEAWAYS

- If you view your community as your achievement, you will be drained by it. If you view it as something that is owned by many, and not only tied to your worth, you will be recharged by it.
- It is an event organizer's responsibility to consider who their gathering is for. If their audience isn't as diverse as they want, it is their job to take steps to bring in the type of people they want to attract. While this is uncomfortable work, it's also necessary.
- In order to prevent burnout, community builders need to prioritize taking care of themselves and establish a culture where that is encouraged. Asking for help should be normal and praised.

QUESTIONS TO CONSIDER

- How can community builders be more financially rewarded for their work?
- What tactics can gatherers use to conserve their energy and engage in more self-care?
- What tools can we create, which make it easier for gatherers to ask for help?

9

WRAPPING THINGS UP

"What makes a community or individual resilient is not self-mastery or will—it is the quality, strength, and inclusivity of our relational bonds."

—LUCIÉN DEMARIS

Right before I finished this book, I went on a five-day therapy retreat with my family. It was the most intense thing I have ever done. We were in session for seven hours a day, which was as difficult and draining as you imagine. Plus, since all of us were staying in separate hotels, I had no one to spend time with at night for almost an entire week. I felt deeply alone and more emotionally raw than I had ever been in my entire life. At any moment I was one cute puppy picture or Enya song away from a mental breakdown.

Thankfully, I took my own advice and asked my community for help before I left. I told my friends that I was about to venture into scary territory and asked them to reach out while I was gone. "Even if I don't respond," I said, "keep sending me animal GIFs and love notes. I can't get through this on my own. I'm scared."

Even though I was physically alone that week, I had a virtual congregation to protect me. In the mornings I had friends call me, in the afternoon they sent me videos telling me they supported me, and at night they Facetimed me and sent voice messages back and forth. (Also, pictures of golden retriever puppies and baby bunnies were flowing 24/7.) Mike sent me a text listing all the reasons why he admired me. Duncan said a prayer for me multiple times. Oliver took my mind off things by diving into the amazing details of his week.

One particular therapy session was really tough. I was sobbing and didn't think I could handle another minute. But then I did something my therapist recommended. I imagined my entire community standing in a circle around me. It might sound crazy, but picturing them there with me was the only reason I got through that week. I don't think I could have dealt with it otherwise.

The day I was heading back to New York, I sent my friend Amanda a message. "I'm coming home from the airport!" I said. "When I get back, I'd absolutely love to snuggle some of my friends. Can you help me with that?" "Say no more!" she responded.

So, at 10 p.m. on a Tuesday, I rolled my suitcase into an apartment filled with people I love. They yelled, "Group hug!" and surrounded me, squeezing me as tightly as they could. I immediately started crying.

"This week has been so hard," I told them. "So, so hard." My friends just squeezed me harder, letting me cry as they silently supported me.

"You're a warrior," Matt said. With that, we all plopped onto some cushions, snuggled against each other, and talked about other things. We ate Japanese candy, and laughed, and had a mini dance party. Throughout that entire week, my community truly felt like a healthy congregation—and they saved me.

I decided to write *Unlonely Planet* because I want to destigmatize loneliness and provide a framework for anyone to find and create their own healthy congregation. As a refresher, those steps are:

1. **Getting frientimate**—Deepen the intimacy in all of your relationships rather than romantic partnerships alone. This will make you far happier and more connected.
2. **Creating an alternate universe**—Take the time and energy to find spaces that make you a better version of yourself. These gatherings will help you find people who share your values.
3. **Sharing with strangers**—Find gatherings that allow you to have conversations with people you don't know. Sharing with strangers is a way to feel connected to others, reduce shame around what you're dealing with, and remember that you're not alone.
4. **Seeking spiritual guidance**—Look for people who can guide you on your path, spiritually or otherwise. Three effective ways to promote this type of mentorship are creating intergenerational spaces, modeling new forms of spiritual leadership, and creating community hubs.
5. **Finding healing spaces**—Prioritize spaces that can help you heal from your trauma. While this is difficult work, it is the biggest gift you can give yourself.
6. **Incorporating ritual**—Participate in collective song, dance, and storytelling. These experiences will help you feel connected to others and also serve as powerful tools to fall back on in times of tragedy.
7. **Stepping into leadership**—Create the spaces you want to see in the world. Gathering people is one of the best ways to feel connected to your purpose and your community.

You hold the power to create rich and rewarding connections in your own life. Yes, doing that is vulnerable. And just like in dating, finding your community involves its fair share of disappointments. You will attend some events and feel like you wasted your time. You'll reach out to someone you're sure will be an amazing new friend and never hear back. You'll wonder if you'll ever feel like you belong. Yet this is part of the process. If it was easy, it wouldn't be as meaningful when you finally have the connections in your life that you always craved.

I hope this book inspires you to be a gatherer. People are hungry for connection everywhere you go. By creating spaces intentionally, you will not only help others but strengthen your own sense of connection to your community. Becoming a gatherer has been the biggest gift of my life, and it's one I hope you give yourself. Fingers crossed, *Unlonely Planet* will give you the tools to step into that role with a little more confidence.

Right now, the people who create connection are not valued enough. I hope that changes. They give their heart and soul to community building, but don't have enough resources. If we want to prevent our gatherers from burning out, we need to give back to them—especially financially.

I hope the "questions to consider" throughout this book have sparked some ideas for making the world a less lonely place. I would love to have a global conversation about how to make that happen. If you're interested, email hey@joylist.nyc. Let's create some connection, shall we?

Highest of fives and warmest of hugs,

Jillian

REFERENCES

1 (Pew Research Center 2019) Pew Research Center. 2019. "Religious Landscape Study." https://www.pewforum.org/religious-landscape-study/

2 (Walker and McKee 2013) Walker, Tim and Alia McKee. 2013. "The State of Friendship in America 2013: A crisis of confidence." Lifeboat, May 21, 2013. chrome-extension://oemmndcbldboiebfnladdacbdfmadadm/https://static1.squarespace.com/static/5560cec6e4b0cc18bc63ed3c/t/55625cabe4b0077f89b718ec/1432509611410/lifeboat-report.pdf

3 (Polack 2018) Polack, Ellie. 2018. "New Cigna Study Reveals Loneliness at Epidemic Levels in America." Cigna, May 01, 2018.

4 (World Health Organization 1994) World Health Organization. 1994. "Global Strategy on Occupational Health For All: The Way to Health at Work." https://www.who.int/occupational_health/publications/globstrategy/en/index2.html

5 (Tiwari 2013, 320-322) Tiwari, Sarvada Chandra. 2013. "Loneliness: a Disease?" Indian Journal of Psychiatry 55(4): 320-322. https://doi.org/10.4103/0019-5545.120536.

6 (Merriam-Webster, n.d.) Merriam-Webster. N.d. "Congregate Verb." https://www.merriam-webster.com/dictionary/congregate

7 (Voce 2016) Voce, Baya. "The Simple Cure for Loneliness," Youtube Video, "TEDx Talks," October 7, 2016, https://www.youtube.com/watch?v=KSXh1YfNyVA.

8 (Hsu 2018) Hsu, David T. 2018. "Untethered: A Primer on Social Isolation." https://www.readuntethered.com/

9 (Hari 2018) Hari, Johann. Lost Connections: Why You're Depressed and How to Find Hope. Bloomsbury USA, 2018

10 (Hari 2018) Hari, Johann. 2018. "We Know Junk Food Makes Us Sick. Are 'Junk Values' Making Us Depressed?." Los Angeles Times, January 21, 2018. https://www.latimes.

com/opinion/op-ed/la-oe-hari-kasser-junk-values-20180121-story.html

11 (Junger 2016) Junger, Sebastian. Tribe: On Homecoming and Belonging. Twelve, 2016.

12 (World Health Organization 2009) World Health Organization. 2009. "Mental Health, Poverty and Development." ECOSOC. chrome-extension://oemmndcbldboiebfnladdacbdfmadadm/https://www.who.int/nmh/publications/discussion_paper_en.pdf.

13 (Nelson 2017) Nelson, Shasta. "Frientimacy: The 3 Requirements of All Healthy Friendships," Youtube Video, "TEDx Talks," December 15, 2017, https://www.youtube.com/watch?v=hmJyWreER7A.

14 (Baer 2017) Baer, Drake. 2017. "There's a Word For The Assumption That Everybody Should Be in a Relationship." The Cut, March 8, 2017. https://www.thecut.com/2017/03/amatonormativity-everybody-should-be-coupled-up.html

15 (Brake 2012) Brake, Elizabeth. Minimizing Marriage: Marriage, Morality, and the Law (Studies in Feminist Philosophy). Oxford University Press USA, 2012.

16 (Coontz 2006) Coontz, Stephanie. 2006. "How To Stay Married." https://www.stephaniecoontz.com/articles/article34.htm

17 (Jorgensen 2016) Jorgensen, Sydney. 2016. "Sociologists Say Married People Need Friends Too." The Daily Universe, May 3, 2016. https://universe.byu.edu/2016/05/03/sociologists-say-relationships-should-exist-outside-of-marriage/

18 (Hummus 2018) Hummus (@piccaaso). 2018. "does anyone else feel 'touch deprived?' & I'm not talking about touching in a sexual way but simple platonic gestures like hugs, having someone play with your hair, resting your head on someone's shoulders and so on..no one prepared me for how lonely adult-friendships really are." Twitter post, September 10, 2018. https://twitter.com/piccaasso/status/1039298333167243264

19 (Ducharme 2018) Ducharme, Jamie. 2018. "Science Says You Should Embrace Hugging." Time, October 3, 2018. http://time.com/5413957/hugs-are-good-for-you/

20 (Delgado, n.d.) Delgado, Jennifer. N.d. "Why Does Our Brain Needs At Least 8 hugs A Day?." Psychology Spot. https://psychology-spot.com/brain-needs/

21 (Roth 1992) Roth, Geneen. When Food Is Love: Exploring the Relationship Between Eating and Intimacy. Plume, 1992.

22 (The 5 Love Languages 2019) The 5 Love Languages. 2019. "5 Love Languages." https://www.5lovelanguages.com/

23 (Poswolsky 2017) Poswolsky, Smiley. 2017. "The Man Who Gave Us All the Things." Medium, January 12, 2017. https://medium.com/dear-levi/the-man-who-gave-us-all-the-things-e83ab612ce5c

24 (The Get Down, n.d.) The Get Down. "Home." https://www.thegetdownnyc.com/

25 (Thurston and Kuile 2017) Thurston, Angie and Casper Kuile. 2017. "How We Gather." https://static1.squarespace.com/static/5a32a872ace8649fe18ae512/t/5a6f3b9bec212de83ac81b77/1517239214228/How_We_Gather_Digital_4.11.17.pdf

26 (Kuile and Thurston, n.d.) Kuile, Casper and Angie Thurston. N.d. "Something More." https://static1.squarespace.com/static/5a32a872ace8649fe18ae512/t/5a6f3c05652dea28ba274e5f/1517239308968/Something+More_F_Digital_Update.pdf

27 (Inc. Magazine 2016) Inc. Magazine. 2016. "How Tony Robbins Created an Empire by Being the Most Confident Man on Earth." Inc. https://inc.com/magazine/201610/most-confident-man-tony-robbins.html.

28 (Cacioppo and Patrick 2009) Cacioppo, John T. and William Patrick. Loneliness: Human Nature and the Need for Social Connection. W. W. Norton & Company, 2009.

29 (Brown 2015) Brown, Brené. Daring Greatly: How the Courage to Be Vulnerable Transforms the Way We Live, Love, Parent, and Lead. Avery, 2015.

30 (Huffman, n.d.) Huffman, Sara. N.d. "Study: We Communicate Better with Strangers Than Friends, Spouses." Consumer Affairs. https://www.consumeraffairs.com/news04/2011/01/study-we-communicate-better-with-strangers-than-friends-spouses.html.

31 (Brown 2017) Brown, Brené. Braving the Wilderness: The Quest for True Belonging And the Courage To Stand Alone. Random House, 2017.

32 (Bishop 2009) Bishop, Bill. The Big Sort: Why the Clustering of Like-Minded America is Tearing Us Apart. Mariner Books, 2009.

33 (Epley and Schroeder 2014) Epley, N. and Schroeder, J. 2014. "Mistakenly Seeking Solitude." Journal of Experimental Psychology: General, 143(5), 1980-1999.

34 (Markman 2014) Markman, Art. 2014. "Why You Should Talk to Strangers." Psychology Today, November 19, 2014. https://www.psychologytoday.com/us/blog/ulterior-motives/201411/why-you-should-talk-strangers

35 (United States Institute of Peace 2004) United States Institute of Peace. 2004. "What Works? Evaluating Interfaith Dialogue Programs." Special Report, July, 2004. https://www.usip.org/sites/default/files/sr123.pdf

36 (Griffiths 2004) Griffiths, Lawn. "Author Finds Feminism, Independence Among Nuns." Unveiled, March 6, 2004. http://www.nunsunveiled.com/review_030604.html.

37 (Radical Grace 2015) Parrish Rebecca. Radical Grace. DVD. Directed by Rebecca Parrish. United States of America: Interchange Productions, 2015.

38 (Civic Enterprises and Hart Research Associates 2014) Civic Enterprises and Hart Research Associates. 2014. "The Mentoring Effect: Young People's Perspectives on the Outcomes and Availability of Mentoring." MENTOR, January 2014. https://www.mentoring.org/new-site/

wp-content/uploads/2015/09/The_Mentoring_Effect_Full_Report.pdf.

39 Kuile, Casper ter, Angie Thurston and Sue Phillips. N.d. "Care of Souls." chrome-extension://oemmndcbldboiebfnladdacbdfmadadm/https://static1.squarespace.com/static/5a32a872ace8649fe18ae512/t/5c54fd3f4785d36b23f6dc37/1549074027946/Care+of+Souls.pdf.

40 (Hoffower 2019) Hoffower, Hillary. 2019. "Millennial Tech Workers Are Paying $5,000 for a 1-Week Luxury Retreat to Feel Younger, And It Shows Just How Bad Ageism In Silicon Valley Really Is." Business Insider, March 7, 2019. https://www.businessinsider.com/luxury-retreat-modern-elder-academy-tech-workers-millennials-silicon-valley-ageism-2019-3

41 (Lindsey 2011) Lindsey, Elizabeth. 2011. "Wisdom Is Found In Our Heritage, Not Our Cell Phones." TED, March 20, 2011. http://www.cnn.com/2011/OPINION/03/20/lindsey.native.explorers/index.html

42 (Weber 2018) Weber, Jeremy. 2018. "Pew: Why Americans Go to Church or Stay Home." Christianity Today, August 1, 2018. https://www.christianitytoday.com/news/2018/july/church-attendance-top-reasons-go-or-stay-home-pew.html.

43 (UK Men's Sheds Association 2019) UK Men's Sheds Association. "Home." 2019. https://menssheds.org.uk/.

44 (Block 2009) Block, Peter. Community: The Structure of Belonging. Berrett-Koehler Publishers, 2009.

45 (Kolk 2015) Kolk, Bessel van der. The Body Keeps The Score: Brain, Mind, and Body in the Healing of Trauma. Penguin Books, 2015.

46 (ACEs Too High News 2019) ACEs Too High News. "Got Your ACE Score?". Last modified 2019. https://acestoohigh.com/got-your-ace-score/.

47 (Stevens et al., n.d.) Stevens, Jane Ellen, Daniel Molina, Kirsti Thompson and Andrew Ventura. 2019. "Beyond Trauma: Building Resilience to Adverse Childhood Experiences." Interface Children Family Services, 2019. https://www.acesconnection.com/g/first-5-association-statewide-trauma-informed-care-collaborative/fileSendAction/fcType/0/fcOid/470531328527800990/filePointer/470531328527801030/fodoid/469827259633357979/Beyond%20Trauma%20-%20Building%20Resilience%20to%20ACEs.pdf.

48 (The Work 2017) The Work. DVD. Directed by Jairus McLeary. United Kingdom, 2017. https://www.imdb.com/title/tt5836866/

49 (Shira 2017) Shira, Gabriel, Valenti J, Naragon-Gainey K and Young AF. 2017. "The Psychological Importance of Collective Assembly: Development and Validation of the Tendency for Effervescent Assembly Measure (TEAM)." Psychol Assess 29(11):1349-1362. https://www.ncbi.nlm.nih.gov/pubmed/28263640

50 (Baer 2017) Baer, Drake. 2017. "Protests, Parties, and Sports Games All Fill the Same Human Need." New York the Cut, January 23, 2017. https://www.thecut.com/2017/01/why-being-part-of-a-crowd-feels-so-good.html

51 (Pearce, Launay and Dunbar 2015) Pearce Eiluned, Launay Jacques and Dunbar Robin I. M. 2015. "The Ice-Breaker Effect: Singing Mediates Fast Social Bonding" Royal Society Open Science, October 1, 2015. http://doi.org/10.1098/rsos.150221

52 (Weinstein et al. 2016) Weinstein, Daniel Alan, Jacques Launay, Eiluned Pearce, Robin I M Dunbar and Lauren Stewart. "Singing and Social Bonding." 2016. 10.1016/j.evolhumbehav.2015.10.002.

53 (Woodward 2017) Woodward, Aylin. "With a Little Help from My Friends." Scientific American, May 1, 2017. https://www.scientificamerican.com/article/with-a-little-help-from-my-friends/

54 (Zauzmer 2017) Zauzmer, Julie. "A Scientist's New Theory: Religion Was Key To Humans' Social Evolution." The Washington Post, February 27, 2017. https://www.washingtonpost.com/news/acts-of-faith/wp/2017/02/27/a-scientists-new-theory-religion-was-key-to-humans-social-evolution/?utm_term=.926df6cbdb12.

55 (SWR1RP 2018) "Flashmob - Sound of Silence: Disturbed," Youtube Video, "SWR1RP," August 29, 2018, https://www.youtube.com/watch?v=Roes_HMog1c.

56 (Bietti, Tilston and Bangerter 2018) Bietti, Lucas M., Ottilie Tilston and Adrian Bangerter. "Storytelling as Adaptive Collective Sensemaking." Wiley Online Library, 28 June, 2018. https://doi.org/10.1111/tops.12358.

57 (Tatum 2003) Tatum, Beverly Daniel. Why Are All The Black Kids Sitting Together in the Cafeteria: and Other Conversations About Race. Basic Books, 2003.

58 (Parker 2018) Parker, Priya. The Art of Gathering: How We Meet And Why It Matters. Riverhead Books, 2018.

59 (Maslach et al., n.d.) Maslach, Christina, Susan E. Jackson, Michael P. Leiter, Wilmar B. Schaufeli and Richard L. Schwab. "Maslach Burnout Inventory." Mind Garden. 2019. https://www.mindgarden.com/117-maslach-burnout-inventory

60 (Sato 2014) Sato, kai. "Why the 5 People Around You Are Crucial to Your Success." Entrepreneur Europe, May 9, 2014. https://www.entrepreneur.com/article/233444.

61 (Silver 2017) Silver, LiYana. Feminine Genius: The Provocative Path to Waking Up and Turning On The Wisdom of Being A Woman. Sounds True, 2017.

62 (Palmer 2017) Palmer, Parker J. The Courage To Teach: Exploring the Inner Landscape of a Teacher's Life. Josey-Bass, 2017.

Printed in Great Britain
by Amazon